# CULTURES OF THE WORLD®

# BELARUS

## Patricia Levy and Michael Spilling

 **Marshall Cavendish**
Benchmark

New York

D0010230

**PICTURE CREDITS**

Cover photo: © Ottmar Bierwagen / Spectrum Photo File

alt.TYPE / REUTERS: 110 • ANA Press Agency: 3 • Bjorn Klingwall: 29, 69, 72, 81 • Bruce Coleman Ltd: 38, 42, 84, 125 • Corbis: 1, 51, 53, 57, 116, 127 • ELTA: 20 • Getty Images: 6, 49, 52, 54, 55, 63, 66, 91, 98, 103, 107, 124 • Hutchison Library: 13, 82, 101 • Lonely Planet Images: 30, 32, 68, 70, 71, 76, 80, 88, 89, 96, 102, 106, 121 • North Wind Picture Archives: 21 • Novosti: 7, 8, 12, 95, 118, 119 • Novosti (London): 22, 23, 24, 26, 28, 33, 60, 78, 126 • Photolibrary: 5, 39, 44, 45, 48, 50, 58, 61, 74, 93, 130, 131 • Photolibrary / Alamy: 14, 16, 46, 64, 75, 97 • SCR Photo Library: 4, 15, 17, 67, 83, 86, 90, 100, 104 • TopFoto: 27 • TRIP Photographic Library: 9, 11, 36, 40, 41, 43, 47, 59, 65, 73, 77, 99, 108, 109, 112, 113, 117, 123, 128

**PRECEDING PAGE**

Belarusian children reciting their pledge.

Publisher (U.S.): Michelle Bisson
Editors: Deborah Grahame, Mindy Pang
Copyreader: Daphne Hougham
Designer: Benson Tan
Cover picture researcher: Connie Gardner
Picture researcher: Thomas Khoo

Marshall Cavendish Benchmark
99 White Plains Road
Tarrytown, NY 10591
Website: www.marshallcavendish.us

© Times Media Private Limited 1998
© Marshall Cavendish International (Asia) Private Limited 2010
All rights reserved. First edition 1998.
® "Cultures of the World" is a registered trademark of Times Publishing Limited.

Originated and designed by Times Media Private Limited
An imprint of Marshall Cavendish International (Asia) Private Limited
A member of Times Publishing Limited

All Internet sites were correct and accurate at the time of printing. All monetary figures in this publication are in U.S. dollars.

*Library of Congress Cataloging-in-Publication Data*
Levy, Patricia, 1951-
  Belarus / by Patricia Levy and Michael Spilling. — 2nd ed.
     p. cm. — (Cultures of the world)
  Includes bibliographical references and index.
  Summary: "Provides comprehensive information on the geography, history, wildlife, governmental structure, economy, cultural diversity, peoples, religion, and culture of Belarus"—Provided by publisher.
  ISBN 978-0-7614-3411-5
  1. Belarus—Juvenile literature. I. Spilling, Michael. II. Title.
  DK507.56.L48 2009
  947.8—dc22          2008028786

Printed in China

7 6 5 4 3 2 1

# CONTENTS

INTRODUCTION    5

GEOGRAPHY    7
*Climate • Relief • Rivers and lakes • The Pripet Marshes • Flora and fauna • Belavezhskaya Forest Nature Reserve • Cities*

HISTORY    17
*The Slavs • Kievan Rus • The Grand Duchy of Lithuania • Union with Poland • A battleground • Russian rule • Revolution and war • Life in the USSR • World War II and the cold war • Chernobyl • Toward independence • Conflict in the new country*

GOVERNMENT    31
*The president and parliament • Local government • Political parties • The judiciary • Foreign relations*

ECONOMY    39
*Agriculture • Energy • Manufacturing • Natural resources • Transportation*

ENVIRONMENT    49
*Chernobyl—Two decades later • Wildlife and Chernobyl • Endangered animals • National parks • Industrial pollution • Water resources*

BELARUSIANS    59
*Belarusians • Russians • Poles • Jews • Others • National dress • Some famous Belarusians*

LIFESTYLE    69
*Life in the cities • Life in the country • Women and the family • Education • Marriage • Children • Life after Chernobyl*

A war memorial in Belarus. The victim of many wars, including Napoleon's march on Russia in the 1800s, Belarus also suffered the devastation of World War II.

3

**A simple traditional house in the city of Polotsk.**

RELIGION 81
*Early religions • The Orthodox Church • Roman Catholicism • The Uniate Church • Important church figures*

LANGUAGE 89
*Early roots of language • Belarusian • Russian • What's in a name?*

ARTS 97
*Music • Architecture • Religious icons • Crafts, woodcarving, and ceramics • Socialist realism • Literature*

LEISURE 107
*In the outdoors • Storytelling and theater • Entertainment in the cities • Sports • The media*

FESTIVALS 117
*Traditional festivals • Christian festivals • Jewish festivals • Soviet celebrations • Music festivals*

FOOD 125
*Bread • Potatoes • Meat dishes • Kitchens • Sweets and drinks*

MAP OF BELARUS 132

ABOUT THE ECONOMY 135

ABOUT THE CULTURE 137

TIME LINE 138

GLOSSARY 140

FURTHER INFORMATION 141

BIBLIOGRAPHY 141

INDEX 143

# INTRODUCTION

BELARUS BECAME AN INDEPENDENT COUNTRY only as recently as 1991. Previously known as Belorussia (White Russia), under the leadership of President Alexander Lukashenko the country maintains strong economic and cultural links with its much larger neighbor Russia. Some Belarusians seek reunification with Russia, and this remains one of the most important political questions confronting Belarus today. Set amid a region of political and economic liberalization, Belarus nevertheless has retained a state-run economy and Soviet-style politics. Belarus was also ill-fated enough to be heavily exposed to the radioactive fallout from the nuclear explosion at the Chernobyl power plant in neighboring Ukraine in 1986, and almost a quarter of the country remains affected by radiation.

Despite their environmental problems, Belarus is a beautiful country and is home to many national parks sheltering primeval forests and abundant wildlife. It is one of the few places in Europe where rare European bison (wisent), elks, wild boars, wolves, bears, and lynx still roam wild.

The history of Belarus is closely tied to those of its neighbors, Poland, Lithuania, Russia, and Ukraine. This linkage is reflected in the country's rich cultural heritage. This book explores the recent history, economic developments, and the political climate of Belarus, a country that remains at a crossroads in its history.

# GEOGRAPHY

BELARUS IS A SMALL LANDLOCKED COUNTRY in northeastern Europe and forms part of the Great Plain of Eastern Europe. To the northwest are the Baltic republics of Latvia and Lithuania, to the west is Poland, to the east is the Russian Federation, and to the south lies Ukraine. The country has a total area of 80,155 square miles (207,600 square km), which makes it slightly smaller than Kansas in the United States. The population density is fairly low with only about 127 persons per square mile (47 persons per square km).

The landscape of Belarus is mostly flat and was shaped by prehistoric glaciers. Some 37.8 percent of the country is covered with forest, while in the south the plains turn into marshland. An extensive network of rivers and streams courses throughout Belarus, with the heavily used Dnieper River being the largest.

Much of the land has been converted to agricultural farmland with grain, potatoes, vegetables, and flax being the principal crops. At the end of summer, Belarusian fields become seas of blue from the abundant flax flowers.

Unfortunately, much of the south of the country remains uninhabited and unusable since the 1986 nuclear accident at Chernobyl in neighboring Ukraine. The soil is lethally contaminated, and it has affected agriculture as well as the natural forests and wildlife. Despite this colossal accident and the loss of forested areas, Belarus still has a great variety of wildlife compared with other areas in Europe.

*Above:* **A stork nesting atop a telephone pole—part of the diverse wildlife in Belarus.**

*Opposite:* **An autumn-colored forest is reflected on the water of Lake Viacha.**

7

Like much of
the country, the
ridges and hills
in Belarus were
once covered by
forest. They have
long since been
cleared, however,
and converted to
agricultural land.

# CLIMATE

The Belarusian continental climate is relatively dry throughout the year. It has warm summers and very cold winters, with freezing temperatures and continuous snow cover from December to March.

As one travels north and east, the weather becomes increasingly colder and wetter. Summers are cool and moist: average temperatures in July and August, the hottest months, are around 65°F (18°C), while temperatures during January and February range from 18°F to 25°F (–8°C to –4°C).

The warm, moist, westerly winds that cross Europe from the Atlantic Ocean have lost most of their moisture by the time they reach Belarus, so rainfall is moderate, although slightly heavier than much of the rest of Eastern Europe. Annual rainfall ranges from 21 to 28 inches (53–71 cm) with the highest rainfall in the north of the country around the low hills and ridges. Rain is most frequent in the summer months and often delays the harvest of ripened crops.

**An autumn day. These young birches with beautiful white trunks are the first trees to appear as the forest is returned to nature after years of agricultural use.**

## RELIEF

Belarus is part of the Great Plain of Eastern Europe, which stretches from the Ural Mountains in Russia to the Carpathians in the south and west. The landscape is mostly low-lying except for a few high areas of flat-topped hills. These were formed at the end of the last ice age (10,000 years ago) when melting and retreating glaciers left behind huge piles of accumulated rock and soil that are called moraines.

The highest point in the country is Dzyarzhynskaya Mountain in the west, which reaches 1,135 feet (346 m). The largest ridge running all through the country, northeast to southwest,

is the Belarusian Ridge. Another ridge, the Ashmyany Upland, is in the northwest and stretches westward to the city of Vilnius in neighboring Lithuania. Between the ridges lie wide, poorly drained lowlands interspersed with many small lakes. North of the Belarusian Ridge is the Polotsk Lowland, while in the south the Central Berezina Plain gradually slopes toward marshland. The Neman River is the lowest point in the country, at an elevation of 295 feet (90 m).

## RIVERS AND LAKES

The Dnieper River, which for much of its course flows through Belarus, is the fourth-longest river in Europe. It is navigable for most of its

**The Svisloch River, which courses through the capital city of Minsk, is a popular recreation spot.**

*The Dnieper River is an important source of food for many people along its course, containing over 60 species of fish, including carp, catfish, and pike.*

1,367 miles (2,200 km) and drains a total of 195,000 square miles (505,050 square km). It is frozen from November to March, then becomes very full in the spring after the thaw, when it drains meltwater from the surrounding countryside. For Belarusians, the river is an important means of shipping along much of its length, transporting floating timber and barges of coal, ore, and minerals. In northern Belarus, the Dnieper River is joined to the rivers Neman and Western Dvina by canals, and through these arteries Belarus has a hookup to the Baltic Sea. After flowing through the Ukraine, the Dnieper River reaches the Black Sea.

The Pripet is another large river that flows east/southeast to join the Dnieper. Its total length is 480 miles (775 km). Linked by a canal to the Western Dvina River (also known as the Daugava River), the Pripet gives another valuable route to the Baltic Sea. The Berezina, a smaller river, also joins the Dnieper, though it is navigable only by small vessels. The Bug River forms part of the border with Poland, while the Western Dvina arises in Russia and flows through Belarus before finally reaching the Baltic Sea. With its diverse streams, rivers, and canals, Belarus has in all about 20,800 waterways with a total length of some 56,300 miles (90,600 km).

The river routes provide three corridors—the Dnieper runs north to south on its way to the Black Sea; the Western Dvina and Neman drain northern and western Belarus and flow toward the Baltic Sea in the north; and the southwest is drained by the tributaries of the Bug River, which flow to the Baltic Sea as well

There are more than 11,000 lakes scattered throughout the lowlands. Lake Naroch, 31 square miles (80 square km), and Lake Osveyskoye, 22 square miles (58 square km), are the two largest.

## THE PRIPET MARSHES

Covering a total area of 104,000 square miles (270,000 square km) across Belarus and Ukraine, the Pripet Marshes, a wetland area in southern Belarus, was once the largest marshland in Europe. It lies in the basins formed by the rivers Pripet and Dnieper and straddles the Belarus/Ukraine border. The land is flat, with sandy soils crisscrossed by many shallow rivers. The rivers overflow easily and thus the land is constantly flooded or waterlogged. The many lakes in the area are constantly becoming choked with marsh vegetation; as they fill with the plants, more marshland is created. Mixed woodlands of coniferous and deciduous trees grow there abundantly, and the wildlife is especially diverse. It is usually warm and humid in the marshes.

Land reclamation projects were applied in the area during the 20th century, draining the marshes and filling in with soil to make the land dry and stable. The drained and cleared tracts were then converted to agricultural land for crops such as flax, potatoes, and rye. Excavated peat—partially decomposed and carbonized vegetation—is burned as fuel for cooking and heating.

Herds of wild horses live in the marshland of southern Belarus.

*In Belarus the Pripet Marshes are sometimes described as the "lungs of Europe," because the air currents that pass over the area are reoxygenated and purified by the swamps, which absorb carbon dioxide.*

Many animals, including deer (*above*), wild boars, bison, and elks, are thriving within the national parks and nature reserves of Belarus.

## *FLORA AND FAUNA*

Belarus has a generously diversified plant and animal life that has evolved over 10,000 years, since the last ice sheets withdrew from Europe. Conifers such as pine and spruce are dominant in the north, while deciduous species such as oak and hornbeam are more common in the south. There is an enormous range of bog and marsh plants in the marshland, and willow trees grace the river banks.

Voles, otters, beavers, and various types of fowl, such as partridge, grouse, and ducks, can be found around rivers. Wild pigs, wolves, mink, deer, elk, and pine martens make the forests their home. Belarus has several major nature reserves—the Belavezhskaya Forest on the border with Poland and the Pripet Nature Reserve in the south are two large reserves, but several others are also interspersed throughout the country.

## *BELAVEZHSKAYA FOREST NATURE RESERVE*

Lying across the Belarus/Polish border, the Belavezhskaya Forest Nature Reserve is the largest surviving area of primeval forest in Europe. About

## THE WISENT

The European bison, or wisent, which nearly became extinct in the 20th century, is closely related to the American bison, commonly called a buffalo. It lives in herds, as the buffalo does, but differs in its habitat, size, and appearance. The European bison lives in forests rather than on plains. A typical adult male wisent is a massive 9.5 feet (2.9 m) long and weighs between 1,760 and 2,000 pounds (800 and 910 kg). This hardy mammal is slightly smaller than the American buffalo, with shorter horns, but is huge, nonetheless. It is the ancient creature often depicted in prehistoric wall paintings found all over Europe. By 1945 only a small herd of 40 animals remained in the Polish part of the Belavezhskaya Forest Nature Reserve. That was the entire world population of the bison! A breeding program was successfully carried out by the park, and now the numbers of bison have increased to several thousand. Some of these welcome bison have since been sent to other nature reserves in Europe, where they have formed the breeding stock for their species in zoos and parks around the world.

683 square miles (1,769 square km) are within Belarus. In the 12th century, this forest extended from the Baltic Sea to the Bug River and from the Oder River to the Dnieper River, but over the centuries much of the forest was cut down for building and agriculture. Much of its wildlife was widely hunted. After World War II the surviving forest was designated as a nature reserve.

Belavezhskaya Forest has been one of the world's greatest success stories in nature conservation. It was the last stronghold of the European bison. The park carried out a successful breeding program, so that now several thousand of the animals live in the park.

The forest has both conifer and deciduous trees—many of these trees are ancient (350–600 years old) and have grown to exceptional heights of 150 feet (45 m) or more. Most of the forest flora is a mixture of eastern and western European plants. Besides the bison, the forest is home to deer, elks, wolves, boars, and lynx as well as the more common squirrels, hares, foxes, martens, and beavers. Many woodland birds are also observed in this bountiful nature reserve.

*The Belavezhskaya Forest survived largely because it was the private hunting reserve of those in power for many centuries—from European kings to Soviet commissars. The forest has now been declared a biosphere reserve by UNESCO (United Nations Educational, Scientific, and Cultural Organization).*

The modern city center of Minsk, the capital of Belarus.

# CITIES

Most of the cities and towns in Belarus were seriously damaged during World War II, although massive rebuilding took place afterward. Many people migrated to the cities during the Soviet era, raising the urban population from 20 percent in 1945 to about 71 percent today.

**MINSK** is the capital and largest city in Belarus, with a population of about 1.8 million. It is situated among low-lying hills along the Svisloch River. It has at times been part of Poland and Lithuania as well as the USSR (Union of Soviet Socialist Republics) during its history. It is now the administrative center for the Commonwealth of Independent States (CIS), the alliance of former Soviet republics. Along with being a base for major industries, Minsk is a major cultural center with universities, a conservatory of music, sports schools, and several theaters.

**GOMEL**, the second-largest city in Belarus, with a population of about 479,000, is a regional capital and administrative center. It is an ancient city with historical records that date back to the 12th century. When Belarus's railways were built in the late 19th century, Gomel became a major railway junction. It is also an important port on the Dnieper River and is a center for the manufacture of phosphate fertilizers, timber products, agricultural machinery, and shoes.

**BREST** lies on the border with Poland in the southwest of the country and is home to almost 300,000 people. It is one of the busiest border crossings in Europe and has a distinct cosmopolitan atmosphere. Residents of Poland and Belarus frequently go back and forth for shopping and trade expeditions. People are drawn from all over the former Soviet Union to trade and barter goods in what has become a thriving city.

*Many of the most important towns in Belarus lie along river routes, where they have gained prominence because of trade and transportation links.*

**A traditional house in Belarus is plain and unassuming.**

# HISTORY

BELARUS HAS EXISTED as an independent nation only since the breakup of the USSR in 1991. But the country now named Belarus has existed in one form or another for many centuries, although ruled by different great powers in succession. The history of Belarus also chronicles the histories of Poland, Lithuania, Russia, and even Germany, but the enduring link is the sense of nationhood felt by the people of Belarus—their common language and customs and, on many occasions, their shared suffering at the hands of invaders.

Belarus has been inhabited since the Old Stone Age, or the Paleolithic Era, about 2 million years ago, which lasted more than a million years. During that period major climate and other changes occurred affecting the evolution of humans. Toward the end of the era, people lived in caves, had complex tools made of bone or stone, and practiced a natural religion. Archaeological remains of a primitive hunting-gathering society, and of more settled Neolithic farming communities, have been found in Belarus.

*Left:* **A beloved World War II memorial in Vitebsk depicts an advancing squad of soldiers.**

*Opposite:* **The Victory Obelisk in Minsk.**

## THE SLAVS

The first Slavs inhabited the region by the second century A.D. and are known to have traded with the Roman Empire. By the sixth century, the Belarusian Slavs were divided into a number of groups with a common language: the Dregovichi (dre-hav-EE-chi) in the south of modern-day Belarus; the Radzimichi (rad-zim-EE-chi) in the east; the Krivichi (kree-VEE-chi), the largest of the tribes, in the north; and the Drevlyane (dre-vla-ne) in the center. By the eighth century the bands had fully developed and had organized social structures, and the principalities of Polotsk, Pinsk, Slutsk, Minsk, and Turov had been established.

## KIEVAN RUS

The Belarus principalities came under the rule of a powerful Slavic state known as Kievan Rus, based in Kiev (in modern Ukraine) in the mid-ninth century. A trading empire developed, based on the river systems of the area, which linked the great Byzantine capital of Constantinople with Kiev and the Baltic Sea to the north. Many present-day towns in Belarus were established at that time. It is also believed that Christianity came to the region during that busy period, via Kiev, which was the first Eastern European state to accept Christianity.

The principalities of Belarus, although under the kingship of Kiev, were mostly self-governing. Each community had a council of representatives from all the villages in the principality. Those councils made all communal decisions and in times of war elected a prince or a leader.

One of the earliest formed principalities, Polotsk, competed with Kiev for supremacy over the other Belarusian settlements. In 1067 a powerful Polotsk leader, Prince Useslau (Vseslav) the Magician (1044–1101), led an unsuccessful battle against Kievan Rus. Beaten in the battle,

Useslau the Magician was imprisoned in Kiev but then rose to Kiev's aid when the Kievan prince got into difficulties in a war against a southern Ukraine province. Useslau actually ruled Kiev for a few months and then returned home to build a stronger, more powerful Polotsk, which ruled over the other principalities of Minsk, Vitebsk, Orsha, and Slutsk. Prince Useslau also began the building of the cathedral of Polotsk, the first monumental structure to be erected in the territory of Belarus.

## THE GRAND DUCHY OF LITHUANIA

Over the next 200 years the power of Polotsk waned and Kiev again dominated the region. But in 1240 Kiev was invaded by Mongols, and its power, in turn, declined. In the course of the Mongol invasion, many settlements in Belarus were destroyed. The Belarusian population was then absorbed into the expanding Grand Duchy of Lithuania (an Eastern and Central European state from the 13th century until the 18th century), but the people clung to much of their independence. During that time the Belarusian language and the sense of a national identity began to develop.

*During the battle of the Niamiga River in 1067, Prince Useslau completely destroyed the town of Minsk. The account of the prince's siege is the first mention of the town in written records.*

### USESLAU THE MAGICIAN

Ruler of Belarus for more than 30 years, Useslau (Vseslav) the Magician is surrounded by many legends. History tells that he was a magical figure. At his birth, the story goes, he had a mark on his forehead. His mother was told by wizards to put a band around his head, covering the mark. He wore the band, which gave him magical powers, all his life. During daylight hours he was a powerful king and lawgiver, but at night he was believed to become a wolf. He would race each night from Kiev to Tmutarakan, east of Crimea. In the morning the bells of Polotsk would toll for him to return, drawing him home to Kiev.

Vytautas ruled the Grand Duchy of Lithuania from 1392 to 1430. During his reign, the grand duchy reached its largest extent, stretching from the Baltic Sea to the Black Sea.

## *UNION WITH POLAND*

In 1386 a union took place between the thrones of Lithuania and Poland through the marriage of Jogaila (1362–1434), a Lithuanian prince, with Queen Jadwiga (1374–99) of Poland. Poland was a Roman Catholic country and part of the marital settlement was that Lithuania, an Eastern Orthodox country, should adopt Catholicism (the beliefs and practices of the Roman Catholic Church). This upset many Lithuanian nobles and their subject peasants, and only a few of them adopted the new religion.

The union between Poland and Lithuania remained difficult, with a constant threat of disunity within the heart of Belarus and threats of invasion from the east. In 1392 a cousin of Jogaila's, named Vytautas (1350–1430), took over the Belarusian throne, and in an attempt to avoid war, Jogaila handed over the princedom of that region to him.

Vytautas became one of the great rulers of the Lithuanian duchy. He rallied the support of other regions, made peace treaties with the Mongol Tatars in the east, and later led an army against their conqueror, Emperor Tamerlane. Under Vytautas, invasions from Western Europe by Christian crusaders also were repelled. A union between the armies of Vytautas and Jogaila pushed back the Teutonic Knights in the Battle of Tannenberg in 1410. Lithuania extended its territories as far as the Baltic Sea in the west and for a time became the most powerful state in Eastern Europe.

Vytautas wanted an independent Lithuania rather than a union with Poland and in 1429 declared independence from Poland. He died soon afterward, however, and under his son, unification with Poland grew strong again.

There followed years of intrigue, and neither the citizens of Poland nor of Lithuania were happy. The two great religions, Catholicism and Eastern Orthodoxy, continued fighting for control of the states. Belarusian national identity and culture flourished within the greater state of Lithuania, however, and immigrants from many races and religions peacefully settled there, including Muslim Tatars, Jews, and Ukrainians. In 1569 Poland and Lithuania joined together to form the Union of Lublin.

## A BATTLEGROUND

Neighboring Russia was a rising power, and it made repeated attempts to seize the region of Belarus from Lithuania in the 1500s. For half a century, Belarusian towns suffered battles for control between the armies of Lithuania and Moscow, and thousands of people died violently. When Ivan IV (1530–84), called "the Terrible," prince of Moscow, began his campaign to take Lithuania's neighbor, Belarus again was in the middle and was occupied by Russian troops. In 1568 Polotsk became Russian territory after a truce, but it suffered almost complete destruction by fire during the battles. In 1576 the Russians were finally driven out.

For many centuries, Belarusian peasants led lives of hardship and servitude.

Other changes also made the lot of the Belarusian people difficult. The Lithuanian Statutes of 1557 set forth property rights on Lithuanian-controlled lands. They reduced the peasants to serfdom, unable to leave the land that they worked for the landowners. The meager freedom that the peasants had enjoyed before was totally lost.

The 17th century also was marked by wars between nearby large powers that used Belarus as their battlefields. Sweden, Moscow, Poland, Denmark, and Cossacks from the Ukraine, one after another, waged battles

Catherine II ruled the Russian Empire from 1762 to 1796. The miseries of serfdom continued under her, although she introduced reforms in other areas.

on Belarusian soil, looting and burning as they went to prevent the enemy from making use of food or supplies. Poland, after gaining control of the area in the Union of Lublin, banned the Belarusian language in official contexts in 1697.

Belarus continued to be involved in wars not of its own making. Napoleon invaded Russia in 1812, and the escape route of his defeated French troops led directly through Belarus.

## RUSSIAN RULE

In 1773, under the pretext of coming to the aid of Orthodox citizens, Russia invaded Belarus yet again. The area of Belarus up to the Dnieper River became part of Russian territory. In 1793 a second Russian invasion took the rest of Belarus as well as northern Ukraine.

Russian rule hardly improved the life of the Belarusian peasants. While wars ceased to be fought on Belarusian soil for the first time in 200 years, the native language and religion were discouraged and a process of Russification began. The universities in Polotsk and Vilnius were closed. The position of Great Prince of Lithuania was eliminated, and the Lithuanian Statutes, the laws that had governed Belarus, were abolished. Belarus was divided into provinces—Minsk, Mogilev, Vilnius, and Vitebsk. Nevertheless, despite Russia's best efforts to assimilate Belarus, Belarusian culture continued to flourish. More than 1.5 million people emigrated from Belarus in the early 1800s in search of economic prosperity and freedom, carrying the Belarusian culture and language with them.

In the 1860s serfdom in the Russian Empire was finally abolished. Small-scale industries were set up, and in the 1880s railway construction began.

## RUSSIFICATION

Russification was a name given to a government policy of Czar Alexander III (1845–94). The policy was intended to bind together all the various peoples in Imperial Russia with a single notion of Russianness. The czar would be the focal point of this new national identity.

Russification was first developed by Count Sergey Uvarov (1786–1855) in the reign of Czar Nicholas I. Count Uvarov set out three principles for Russification: "Orthodoxy, Autocracy, and Nationality." Before the policy of Russification, the various ethnic groups had been left to themselves and were recognized on their own terms, provided they acknowledged their allegiance to the Russian state (the czar) and the Orthodox Church. Under Alexander III, Uvarov's principles became the cornerstone of public education policy. Alexander's government sought to extract a sense of Russian identity from the many different ethnic groups that would supersede any sense of local or ethnic identity—being "Russian" was promoted over being, for example, a Cossack, Estonian, or Kazak. The Soviet regimes of the twentieth century—especially that of Stalin—continued the policy of promoting a broader national identity over local and ethnic identities.

## *REVOLUTION AND WAR*

In 1863 a wide-scale rebellion led by Kastus Kalinouski (1838–64) against the czar broke out all across the Russian Empire, including Belarus. The rebellion was crushed within a year. Kalinouski was executed, and the peasants' desires for greater freedom and for the elimination of the class system

The 1905 Russian Revolution is illustrated in *Death in the Snow*, a forceful painting by Marovsky.

23

were terminated. Building on the peasants' flickering hopes in 1898, the first Marxist party, the Russian Social Democratic Labor Party, was established in Minsk. In the first Russian revolution, in 1905, Belarusian peasants also joined the uprising against the Russian monarchy.

During World War I (1914–18), Belarus again became a battlefield. Vilnius in western Belarus (today in Lithuania) was occupied by German troops. With Russia mired in the midst of a bloody revolutionary war, Belarus declared its independence and for the first time in history became a completely independent state, although somewhat smaller in area than modern Belarus.

Its independence was brief: in 1919 the land was recaptured by Russian communist forces and redesignated the Byelorussian Soviet Socialist Republic. Later that year Belarus merged with Lithuania to form the short-lived region of Litbel. Then a war broke out between Russia and Poland, again fought on Belarusian soil. In 1921, in the Treaty of Riga, Russia ceded large areas of "independent" Belarus to Poland. In 1922 what remained of independent Belarus became one of the signatories of the Union of Soviet Socialist Republics (USSR). As the Belorussian Soviet Socialist Republic, its fleeting independence had ended. Western Belarus, meanwhile, remained under Polish control.

## LIFE IN THE USSR

Although Belarus remained a republic, the Belarusian Soviet Socialist Republic, with a certain amount of autonomy, its central government was in Moscow. The country's intellectual elite happily threw themselves into the new socialist way of life. For several years the language, culture, and sense of identity in Belarus flourished, while the cities grew and people flocked from the countryside to the towns in search of work.

By the 1930s, however, under the dictatorship of Joseph Stalin (1879–1953), there were purges of intellectuals, many thousands of whom were shot or sent to labor camps in Siberia. Collective farms were created, and tens of thousands of farmers were sent away from Belarus to camps or even killed. During this early period of Stalin's rule it is estimated that over a million Belarusians lost their lives. Meanwhile, the 4 million Belarusians who found themselves under Polish rule fared little better. The Belarusian language was prohibited, schools were closed, and political organizations were hunted down and destroyed.

## WORLD WAR II AND THE COLD WAR

At the start of World War II, Stalin signed a nonaggression agreement with Nazi leader Adolf Hitler in Germany. They divided Eastern Europe between them, with the result that western Belarus (which was in Poland's hands at that time) was returned to the USSR. The pact failed, however, and in June 1941 German troops invaded Belarus as part of a wider invasion of the USSR. Germany's occupation and eventual retreat destroyed thousands of ancient buildings, ruined most of the industry, and devastated the farming system. It is estimated that about one million Belarusian people, around 25 percent of the population, perished during the German occupation,

*The Russian Revolution (1917) was a series of economic and social upheavals in Russia, involving first the overthrow of the czarist autocracy, followed by the expulsion of the liberal and moderate-socialist Provisional Government, resulting in the establishment of Soviet power under the control of the Bolshevik party. This eventually led to the consolidation of the Soviet Union in 1922, which survived until its dissolution in 1991.*

*Opposite:* **Joseph Stalin, premier of the USSR from 1941 to 1953, was a brutal dictator.**

Millions died as entire Belarusian villages were destroyed by invading German troops in 1942.

*One of the most famous defenses of World War II happened in the 19th-century citadel in Brest, in June 1941, wherein two Soviet army regiments held the German invaders at bay for nearly a month before surrendering after running out of supplies.*

including almost all of the country's Jewish population. That enormous assault matched Stalin's own a decade earlier.

At the end of the war, in 1945, western Belarus remained part of the Soviet Union, but the many Poles who had settled there between 1921 and 1942 were forcibly deported back to Poland. Vilnius, handed over to Lithuania at the start of the war, never again became part of Belarus. In the postwar years, large numbers of ethnic Russians settled in Belarus.

After the war, plans for economic reform were reinstated, and Belarus became a model for Soviet economic expansion. Massive growth of towns took place, while rural areas declined. Belarus became one of the most prosperous regions in the Soviet Union. Although it had little in the way of natural resources, great industrial machine factories were established in Belarus to supply the rest of the USSR and the world. Its strategic position, on the border of the USSR, with hundreds of miles of forest, also made it an important military site. Many missile bases were set up there.

## CHERNOBYL

In April 1986 the unimaginable happened. A nuclear reactor at Chernobyl (Chornobyl in Belarusian) in the Ukraine, on the border with Belarus, exploded, hurling vast clouds of radioactive dust, the equivalent of 150 Hiroshima bombs, northward into Belarus. Of the radioactive fallout, 70 percent hit Belarus. Two and a half million Belarusians were directly affected by the catastrophe, and the clouds spread to cover the whole of the country. One-fifth of the total landmass of Belarus became a zone of radioactive contamination. The government acted slowly in evacuating thousands of people from the immediate area and building satellite towns around the major cities to relocate them.

Large areas of land in Belarus remain contaminated. People continue to suffer health problems; children have been particularly affected. Farmers desperate for land continue to plant on contaminated soil and graze animals there. Thus food with unsafe levels of radiation makes its way to other parts of the country.

Three days after the nuclear reactor explosion at Chernobyl, that released massive amounts of radioactivity into the atmosphere. The reactor core was later encased in a large concrete and steel structure, but there has been concern recently over cracks developing in the wall. A safer shelter is now being built.

## TOWARD INDEPENDENCE

During the 1980s great changes took place in the USSR under Mikhail Sergeyevich Gorbachev's new policies. They had little impact at first on Belarus, one of the least liberal of the Soviet republics. A demonstration in 1988 was firmly squelched by the authorities, but the next year the Belarusian Popular Front (BPF, a political party created in Belarus during the perestroika [restructuring] and glasnost [openness] times) was established in Vilnius, Lithuania. The BPF successfully campaigned to have the Belarusian language reestablished in schools. The Belarusian Democratic Bloc, a party of all the opposition groups, carried the banner for independence. In July 1990 the Supreme Soviet, the Belarusian parliamentary council, declared independence. It did not become a reality, however, until 1991 when the leaders of the Supreme Soviet were forced to resign and a more moderate chairperson, Stanislav Shushkevich, took their place. Communist parties in Belarus were banned. Later that year the Soviet Union itself was dissolved. On August 25, 1991, Belarus declared itself an independent state.

## CONFLICT IN THE NEW COUNTRY

Despite the newfound independence, conservative elements remained in control of the governing body, the Supreme Soviet. Communist political parties regrouped and were registered as official parties once again. A coalition began campaigning for reintegration with Russia. Politics rapidly developed into two groups, those who wanted to retain independence and those who wanted integration with their larger and more powerful neighbor. The proposed new constitution contained elements making Belarusian the national language and allowing for private ownership of industry, and included several laws concerning human rights. Nonetheless, this was opposed by the conservative majority.

In 1994 Alexander Lukashenko (b. 1954) became the country's first president in independent elections. Lukashenko has remained in office since that time, winning landslide election victories in 2001 and 2006. President Lukashenko has steadfastly opposed privatization of the economy, and private business is still virtually nonexistent. The state continues to control most of the economy.

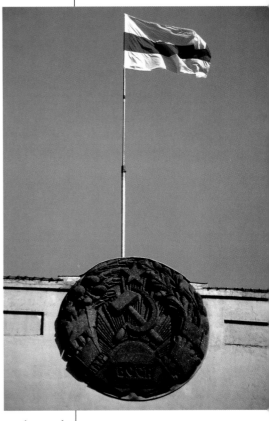

**When Belarus first became independent of the USSR, it adopted this new flag, with plain red and white stripes. It has since changed back to the old Soviet-era flag, which is red and green, with an ornamental stripe.**

Throughout this time, opposition parties have been harassed amid claims of unfair electoral practices, and antigovernment demonstrations in Minsk in 2006 were firmly broken up by the police. Despite opposition to his rule, Lukashenko is popular in rural areas. Belarus remains close to its old master, Russia, and relies on subsidized Russian gas and oil for much of its energy supplies. The two countries retain close military ties, and Lukashenko has initiated negotiations to unify Belarus with Russia into a single state.

# GOVERNMENT

MODERN BELARUS IS A PRESIDENTIAL REPUBLIC, wherein the president is both the head of state and head of government. Executive power is wielded by the government, while legislative power resides with the government and a two-chamber parliament. The only true independence Belarus experienced was the short interval after the breakup of the Soviet Union in 1991. Prior to 1991 various parts of Belarus had at different times been joined to the USSR, the Russian Empire, Germany, Poland, Kievan Rus, and the Grand Duchy of Lithuania.

Before the breakup of the USSR, Belarus had been the most Russified of all the Soviet states. Its language is similar to Russian and so was easily assimilated, and its government was one of the least liberal in the Soviet Union. Throughout the 1990s, after independence from the USSR, political groups in Belarus were in conflict over how the state should be run. The staunch old Communists and President Lukashenko wanted Belarus to remain a socialist state, with state-owned industries and a possible reintegration with Russia. In contrast, many young Belarusians want the economy set free from government control and a more liberal style of government introduced. But many Belarusians grew up in a wealthy Soviet state with full employment and state health care and housing. On the other hand, since 1991, they have come to associate independence with unemployment, closed factories, long lines for food, poor health care, and crumbling public housing. Other groups, who have strong links with Russian nationalist movements, want reintegration with Russia. Russia remains very influential in Belarus, especially because it supplies subsidized oil and gas that are crucial to Belarus's economy and infrastructure.

*Above:* **The national emblem of Belarus, like its flag, has undergone considerable debate in the last few years and its design has been changed several times.**

*Opposite:* **A man walking toward the KGB headquarters on Independence Avenue in Minsk.**

**People walking by the starkly linear Palace of the Republic in Minsk.**

## THE PRESIDENT AND PARLIAMENT

Stanislav Shushkevich led Belarus as chairman of the Supreme Soviet after independence in 1991. He held this position until 1994, when the Supreme Soviet adopted a constitution creating the office of president, who would be the head of government, instead of the prime minister being at the helm. In the following election, the first in the independent state, Alexander Lukashenko was elected as Belarus's first president. Lukashenko was reelected in 2001 and most recently in 2006.

In 1996 Lukashenko held a referendum, the results of which gave him considerably greater powers and that no longer guaranteed the separation of presidential and parliamentary powers in the government. He also disbanded the Supreme Soviet, making way for a two-chamber parliament.

Today, Belarus is a presidential republic governed by the president and a National Assembly. The National Assembly is a two-chamber parliament made up of the 110-member House of Representatives (the lower house) and a 64-member Council of the Republic (the upper house). The House of Representatives is elected by popular vote every four years. The House of Representatives appoints the prime minister of Belarus and—along with the president—controls domestic and foreign policy. In the Council of the Republic, 56 members are appointed by regional councils and 8 are appointed by the president to serve four-year terms. The Council of the Republic selects and appoints government officials and can reject bills passed by the House of Representatives.

Either chamber can veto any law passed by local officials that they consider unconstitutional.

The executive branch of the government of Belarus is a Council of Ministers, headed by a prime minister. This post has been filled by one of Lukashenko's close political allies, Sergei Sidorsky, since 2003. The Council of Ministers forms a governing cabinet, and all members are appointed by the president. The ministers need not be elected members of parliament from the National Assembly.

Parliamentary elections were held in 2000 and 2004. In 2007, 98 of the 110 members of the House of Representatives were independent and not affiliated with any political party. This has been a feature of Belarusian politics, despite the existence of parties that are both for and against President Lukashenko. Voter apathy has hindered the development of a more vibrant democracy. For many years, opposition parties struggled to gain members and support. It was often difficult because so many Belarusians mistrusted the political process and did not believe that democracy would improve their lives. This apathy—in part—contributes to the total dominance of Belarusian politics by Lukashenko and his political allies.

Stanislav Shushkevich was elected chairman of the Supreme Soviet in 1991, in the newly independent Belarus. In 1994, however, he was dismissed after a vote of no confidence.

## LOCAL GOVERNMENT

Under the constitution, Belarus is divided into 6 provinces, or *voblasti* (VOH-blahst-EE), and 141 districts, or *rayoni* (ray-ON-ee), and, below *rayoni*, into cities, towns, and villages. The larger cities are also subdivided into *rayoni*. Each *voblasti* has a legislative authority, called an *oblsovet* (OH-blohs-oh-vet), that is elected by local voters, and a provincial executive administration appointed by the president. In practice, this means local authorities cannot institute any policies that have not been approved by the president's appointed representatives.

*In a referendum held in 2004, the constitution was changed to allow an incumbent to serve an unlimited number of times as president. Previously, a president was limited to two terms.*

## POLITICAL PARTIES

Prior to the liberalization of the USSR, there had been only one political party in Belarus, the Communist Party of Belarus (CPB). It controlled the Supreme Soviet as well as the regional councils. It also supported the 1991 coup in Russia when there was an attempt to remove Mikhail Gorbachev and restore the old Communist system. As a result, the CPB was seriously discredited in Belarus and the party was banned for a period following that upheaval. It found a new way to function in the state by regrouping under the name Party of Communists of Belarus (PCB). There are now several other parties in independent Belarus. Other pro-Lukashenko parties include the nationalist Belarusian Patriotic Party, the Liberal Democratic Party, and the Socialist Sporting Party.

Among opposition parties, the BPF represents the most active opposition group in Belarus. Its goal is a fully independent, democratic Belarus, and it welcomes members of any belief system who share its ideas about independence. Other opposition parties include the United Civic Party (UCP), the PCB, the Green Party, and the Social Democratic Gramada.

In the 2006 election, the main opposition parties formed what was called the "10 Plus Coalition," led by Alexander Milinkevich. Nevertheless, Lukashenko won a massive 82.6 percent of the vote, while the opposition registered a tiny 6 percent. This glaring difference has been questioned by many international observers, who suspect electoral fraud.

## THE JUDICIARY

The independence of the judiciary is no longer guaranteed by the new constitution. The judiciary consists of three courts. The highest is the

Constitutional Court. In this court, half the judges are appointed by the House of Representatives and half by the president. This court can review international treaties, new domestic laws, edicts issued by the president, regulations formulated by the cabinet, aspects of the constitution, and the decisions of the other courts. Its decisions cannot be appealed or taken to a higher court.

Another branch of the court system is the Supreme Court. In the Supreme Court, all the judges are appointed by the president.

The economic courts form the third branch of the system of courts. These courts judge cases involving relations between collective farms, for example, or cases against a monopoly. There is a Supreme Economic Court where decisions in these courts can be appealed.

*Belarus has been barred from membership in the Council of Europe (not to be confused with the European Union) since 1997 for undemocratic voting and election malpractices following the 1996 constitutional referendum.*

## FREEDOM OF SPEECH AND INFORMATION

Many observers have accused the Belarusian authorities of restricting the freedoms of speech and of the press. In elections, opposition politicians have been harassed, as have been the independent media. The government controls most of the printing presses in Belarus, which allows it to severely restrict the publication of opposition newspapers and magazines. The government also controls the sole national television and radio network, meaning that the official version of events goes unchallenged. The United States and the European Union have financed radio, TV, and Internet projects aimed at bringing independent news to people in Belarus, but this so far has had a limited impact, especially as so few Belarusians are connected to the Web.

The government maintains old-style Soviet restrictions of freedom of assembly, requiring anyone who wishes to plan a meeting to apply for permission at least 15 days in advance. Public demonstrations are always closely monitored by the government and security forces.

**A police guard patrolling the streets of a small wet town in Belarus.**

There are also two lower courts, the *voblast*- and *rayon*-level courts. Criminal or civil cases are first heard in the *rayon* courts, which are smaller district courts. The decision of these courts can be taken for review to the *voblast* court. The *voblast* court's decisions can be appealed in the Supreme Court, although these lower court decisions are rarely overturned.

## FOREIGN RELATIONS

Belarus has withstood many invasions and divisions over the course of its history. Many of these changes have come about because of its geopolitical situation. It lies on a flat plain, so any large army wishing to move from east to west or west to east naturally chooses Belarus as the easiest route. Its system of waterways, linking the Baltic Sea with the Black Sea, makes it a strategic target for economic reasons. The country's dense forests and its position as a barrier between Russia and everything west of it made Belarus a perfect site for arms factories and missile bases while it was part of the USSR.

In modern times Belarus is no longer a stronghold against the West, but once again, it is a convenient staging post along the trade routes from Russia to its new Western trading partners. Belarus maintains good relations with its near neighbors, each of whom has owned parts of Belarus at different times and whose ethnic groups form minorities within Belarus today.

Russia has remained Belarus's closest ally and trading partner since the fall of the Soviet Union. Belarus is heavily dependent on Russia for imports of raw materials as well as for all of its energy needs. Impetus for unification of the two countries took a significant step forward with a series of friendship treaties from 1996 to 1999. These treaties called for monetary union, single citizenship, and a common defense and foreign policy. Various trade disputes, however, especially regarding the cost of the subsidized Russian oil and gas that are crucial to Belarus's economy, have put the likelihood of union in doubt. The Russian government maintains superficially friendly relations with the Lukashenko regime, seeing their smaller neighbor as an important buffer against the increasingly pro-Western policies of some of Belarus's neighbors, such as Poland and Lithuania.

Belarus has strained relations with most Western countries, mainly because of its questionable human rights record and government-controlled economy. Belarus has developed strong bonds with Syria, whom it considers to be a key ally in the Middle East, and has begun forging business links with China.

*In 2007 a trade disagreement between the United States and Belarus grew into a diplomatic row that led the United States to impose trade sanctions against Belarusian businesses.*

## COMMONWEALTH OF INDEPENDENT STATES

Belarus belongs to what is known as the Commonwealth of Independent States (CIS). This is a loosely structured grouping of the former Soviet republics, as well as Russia. The capital of the Commonwealth is Minsk in Belarus. Belarus was among the first countries, along with Russia and Ukraine, to sign on to an agreement on December 8, 1991, forming an association among these former republics. There are now 12 members. The Commonwealth is intended to coordinate its various members' activities, including economic undertakings, defense, and foreign relations. In 1993, nonetheless, CIS decided to abandon joint defense, instead to only coordinate military actions. Belarus, Ukraine, and Russia also signed an agreement in 1993 on economic integration. Belarus has agreed to free trade with some of the CIS states.

# ECONOMY

IN BELARUS TODAY MOST OF THE ECONOMY remains in the hands of the state, as in Soviet times, and more than half of the working population works for state-controlled enterprises. Belarus has relatively few natural resources. Newly independent in 1991, it found itself heavily dependent on the other former republics of the USSR for many of its economic needs. The USSR had been, to all intents, a single country for more than 70 years, and so each republic had only a fraction of the resources and industry that it needed to survive alone. Belarus was one of the wealthiest republics in the USSR.

Even after the breakup of the Soviet Union, Belarus continued to prosper, chiefly because it did not immediately undertake the radical changes for becoming a market economy. There were some limited capitalist reforms between 1991 and 1994. Then, following his election victory in the previous year, in 1995 President Alexander Lukashenko began a policy of "market socialism," which allowed the government to regain control of most of the important industries in the country. Business in Belarus is closely managed by the government. The government's socialist policies include the redistribution of wealth by way of high taxes. The government has also sought to maintain high employment by supporting traditional companies and heavily restricting foreign competition. Despite some difficult years, the Belarusian economy grew by 8 percent in 2006, with a total gross domestic product (GDP) of nearly $32 billion. Unfortunately, high inflation eats up much of this growth. Russia remains its largest trading partner, accounting for nearly half of all trade, although commerce with European countries such as Poland and Germany has steadily increased.

*Above:* **A dairy worker processing churned butter in a plant in Brest.**

*Opposite:* **These private flower vendors' stands in Grodno were an early sign of a market economy developing in Belarus.**

*Tourism is still a tiny player in the Belarusian economy, with a scant 100,000 people visiting the country each year. By contrast, Belarusians made more than 12 million visits abroad in 2006.*

# AGRICULTURE

Almost 27 percent of land in Belarus is used for agriculture, and farming accounts for nearly 10 percent of GDP. After World War II, Belarus's agriculture was reorganized into a collective farm system as in the rest of the USSR. These farms used many of the same practices as employed in factories, such as mass production. The state-owned farms were enormous, with tens of families working on each and industrial machines cultivating the fields. Despite some limited privatization since independence, collective farms still occupy more than three-quarters of all agricultural land in Belarus. In addition to these big state farms, small plots of land are allowed to be used by individuals to grow vegetables or raise chickens for home consumption.

A worker milking a cow at a collective farm. Many dairies are located near Minsk.

Following independence, the decision was made to retain this big-farm type of agriculture because so much heavy farm machinery was in place that privately owned small farms could not compete.

Agriculture has always been an important part of the economy in Belarus, but because of the climate, with short summers, only hardy crops can be grown. Many such crops are used as animal feed. The soil is only moderately fertile, but it has been improved with the use of artificial fertilizers. Some of the swampy lowlands have been drained to provide more arable land for fodder crops.

## FARMING AFTER CHERNOBYL

In 1986, after the disastrous nuclear plant accident at Chernobyl in neighboring Ukraine, radioactive fallout fanned by wind spread for hundreds of miles, and much of southern Belarus was contaminated. Before the disaster, this area was the most fertile in Belarus. Altogether, up to 20 percent of agricultural land in Belarus has been affected.

Because of lack of knowledge, the poisoned land regrettably continued to be used long after the disaster, and each time the soil was turned over by plows, more poisonous waste was released into the atmosphere. This unwitting practice continued well into the 1990s. Contaminated crops and animals were shipped all over the country. The government finally intervened, and regional markets set up radiation control centers to check the radioactivity of the meat and vegetables that were being sold.

Forestry, another vital industry, was even more severely hit, with about 20 percent of forestland becoming unusable. Collecting edible forest products, such as mushrooms and fruit, and game hunting for food also became impossible.

Today, the Belarus government wants normal life to return to the damaged areas and is investing heavily in the contaminated region in an attempt to encourage people to work the land and redevelop the area. Special fertilizers have been used to combat the effects of radionuclides in the soil. Only large farms have been able to afford the expensive fertilizers, however, and most small farms continue to operate without it. Cows have been brought into the Gomel region to be bred for their meat, since it proved to be too expensive to produce radiation-free milk. Rapeseed farms have also been developed to help the local farming industry recover.

## FOOD PRICES

Food prices in Belarus are carefully set at levels that people can afford. In the first years of independence, this was done by fixing the prices at which farms could sell their products. This made things very difficult for farms, which could not pass on increasing costs to customers and were often in danger of losing money on their products.

A result of the deliberately low prices in Belarus is that Belarusian food became attractive to neighboring countries. Thus it is exported by local producers who can make a profit by selling abroad. The term "food tourism" came to be an aspect of the Belarusian economy, with foreigners taking vacations in Belarus in order to buy their groceries to take home with them.

*Opposite:* **An oil refinery in Belarus. The country gets much of its crude oil from Russia.**

Potatoes are an important source of food in Belarus. Buckwheat, which does not need much summer heat, is also grown. The seeds are ground into flour or cooked into a kind of porridge. Rye and sugar beets are also widely planted. Smaller amounts of hay, oats, millet, and tobacco are grown, as well as flax and hemp. Most of Belarus's wheat is imported from other former Soviet states, notably Kazakhstan.

Animals are another important aspect of agriculture in Belarus. Pigs and chickens are the most widely raised animals, along with beef cattle.

Generally, grasses, flax, and fodder are grown in the north. Cattle, potatoes, and pigs do well in central Belarus. Hemp farms, cattle, and pastureland predominate in the south.

## ENERGY

Belarus produces most of its own electric power through gas, coal, or oil-fired power stations. Small amounts of peat from the swamplands in the south are also used as fuel. It has a number of small hydroelectric power stations. Belarus is linked through a Soviet electric grid to several other republics but still must import electricity from Russia and Lithuania.

Belarus has suffered a serious fuel crisis since independence. Fuels such as gas and oil that were once freely available from other parts of the USSR suddenly had to be paid for. Ninety percent of Belarus's oil comes from Russia through the Druzhba (Friendship) pipeline, which is the world's longest oil pipeline, carrying oil some 2,500 miles (4,000 km) from southeast Russia to points in Ukraine, Hungary, Poland, and Germany. After several sessions of negotiations and a veiled threat from Russia that new pipelines to the West would be put through Latvia instead of Belarus, an agreement was reached that Russia would supply oil at heavily subsidized domestic rates, while Belarus would export to Russia anything Russia wanted at favorable prices. Russia and Belarus, nevertheless, have been involved in a number of disputes over the cost of the subsidized crude oil.

In 2007 Russia temporarily cut off oil supplies after a disagreement over pricing. Russia wanted Belarus to pay at rates closer to world market prices, in part because Belarus was profiting from the discount. It had been refining the oil it received from Russia and then selling it at a much higher price to other European countries. This dispute will no doubt continue, since Russia intends to steadily raise the cost of oil and gas sold to Belarus in their effort to bring prices in line with the world market by 2011.

A worker fitting a tire onto the wheel of a truck on an assembly line in the Minsk Automobile Plant in Belarus.

## MANUFACTURING

Industry and manufacturing accounts for almost 42 percent of GDP in Belarus. Before World War II, Belarus was largely an agricultural country. The war destroyed most of its farms as well as the modest industry that had existed. After the war the newly reformed socialist republic rebuilt on an industrial base. In some ways the destruction of the factories was an advantage, since the new factories were able to use newer technologies to produce better products at lower prices than their competitors, who were using old prewar machinery. Belarus developed industries concerned with food processing, shoe manufacture, furniture making, linen, textiles, and wood and timber processing.

In the 1970s factories making heavy machinery were introduced. Tractors have been an important export to the other republics and abroad. Other heavy machines produced are trucks, automation machinery, and machine tools. A factory in Gomel, for example, used to produce 90 percent of all self-propelled fodder harvesters in the USSR. Today, Belarus has an important manufacturing sector producing machine tools, tractors, trucks, earthmovers, agricultural equipment, motorcycles, television sets, textiles, radios, and refrigerators. Belarus also has a large chemical processing industry. In Grodno, Gomel, and Soligorsk, fertilizer plants produce mineral fertilizers from nitrates, phosphates, and potassium salts.

# NATURAL RESOURCES

Belarus has few natural resources; the chief one is forestry. There are about 21,750 acres (8,800 ha) of managed forestland. Fir trees predominate in the northern regions of the country, along with birch, black alder, and oak. Replanting projects are helping to increase the total forest reserves. Most timber is harvested and processed in Belarus, while some is directly exported to other countries in the CIS. The wood is used to make furniture and to produce charcoal, a valuable fuel.

Food items such as bilberries, strawberries, and cranberries are harvested along with mushrooms, medicinal plants, and honey from the forests. Some of these products are exported, but most are gathered for the home market. Over 50 types of animals—including deer, elks, ducks, and wild boar—are hunted for food, with about 690 tons (625,957 kg) of such meat yielded per year. A tourist industry that arranges hunting trips for visitors has also recently developed.

Peat, harvested from marshland, is another exploitable natural resource, especially abundant in the Pripet Marshes. It is used as fuel for power stations and for domestic use and also in making fertilizer. There are large deposits of potassium salts, and these are exported to numerous countries. There is also a fertilizer processing company within the country. Table salt is mined on a large scale, while granite is extracted for use in local building projects. Smaller deposits of oil, coal, natural gas, and iron ore are also mined.

Although not rich in minerals, small deposits of iron ore, dolomite, potash (for fertilizer production), rock salt, clay, molding sand, and sand for glass production have been found in Belarus. Belarus also has small quantities of diamonds, titanium, copper ore, nickel, and amber that have yet to be exploited.

A woman spinning fibers into yarn that will later be used to make carpets at a factory in Belarus.

45

**A busy railway station in Belarus.**

## *TRANSPORTATION*

Belarus is in a central location in the transportation grid of Eastern Europe. It is located on a wide, easily navigated plain with central European countries to the west, Scandinavian countries to the north, and the countries of the former USSR to the east and south.

Belarus has approximately 1,550 miles (2,500 km) of waterways, concentrated mostly around the perimeter of the country. The rivers in Belarus have always been an important part of its transportation system. They provide an international trade link between the Black Sea to the south and the Baltic Sea to the north. Belarus benefits from all trade up and down those rivers. The Dnieper–Bug Canal, a shipping canal, was built to connect the Dnieper and Bug rivers flowing to the Black Sea with rivers running to the Baltic Sea, creating a continuous cross-continental route. In 2003 the government began a development program to rebuild and improve the Dnieper–Bug canal locks to bring them up to European standards.

The railways were built in the late 19th and early 20th centuries and form another important link in the transportation system of Belarus, carrying most of its goods to be marketed. There are about 3,420 miles (5,500 km) of railway tracks in the country. The Belarusian Railways manages 21 major railway stations, over 560 local stations and 320 railway junctions. It employs 110,000 people. Minsk, at the center of the system, is linked to Warsaw in Poland and to most other Western European countries. It is also connected directly to Moscow. A north–south line links Saint Petersburg in Russia to Kiev in Ukraine, and a northwest–southeast line leads to Lithuania and Ukraine.

There are 50,500 miles (81,000 km) of paved roads in Belarus. Bus routes connect Belarus with several Polish cities. Other international bus routes, such as the Moscow–Hamburg route, run through Belarus. Minsk, Brest, Vitebsk, Grodno, Gomel, Mogilev, and Bobruisk have electric metropolitan transit systems, either buses or streetcars. Minsk also has an urban railway.

Belarus has international air agreements with 17 countries. There are seven main airports, with two at Minsk and others at Gomel, Brest, Vitebsk, Grodno, and Mogilev.

**Tractors being transported across Belarus by train. Belarus was the third-largest producer of tractors in the world during the 1980s.**

# ENVIRONMENT

IN BELARUS TODAY, THE MAIN ENVIRONMENTAL CONCERNS are chemical and nuclear pollution, both legacies of the country's Soviet past. The colossal accident at the Chernobyl nuclear power plant in 1986 had an enormous impact on Belarus. Northerly winds caused much of the radioactive fallout to settle over farmland in the southeast of the country, primarily around Gomel. Roughly a fifth of Belarus's farmland was affected. Despite assistance from international bodies such as the United Nations (UN), Belarus is suffering still from the consequences of the accident. UN sources estimate that the total cost of dealing with the human, environmental, and economic consequences of the disaster could be as high as $235 billion over a period of 30 years—an enormous sum of money for a small developing country.

*Left:* **An employee of the Belarusian radiation ecology reserve measuring the level of radiation in a village near the Chernobyl explosion.**

*Opposite:* **Though previously damaged by the Chernobyl fallout, this robust tree has been regenerated successfully, and is now growing well.**

The industry of manufacturing heavy machinery, the mainstay of the Belarus economy, has also caused significant air and water pollution. The most common pollutants are formaldehyde, carbon emissions from vehicles, and petroleum chemicals. In 1992 Belarus was among the world's top 50 nations in industrial emissions of carbon dioxide, producing 112.4 million tons (102 million metric tons), or 10.9 tons (9.89 metric tons) per capita. In 1996 the total fell to 68 million tons (61.7 million metric tons). In 2007 Belarus was the 46th most polluting country in the world for carbon dioxide emissions, with 23.7 million tons (21.5 million metric tons). The country's soil also contains unsafe levels of lead, zinc, copper, and the agricultural insecticide dichloro-diphenyl-trichloroethane (DDT). The government has done very little to institute environmentally friendly policies or the necessary laws to protect the environment from further damage.

Despite the environmental damage caused by Chernobyl, however, Belarus has a number of national parks that are home to some of the best-preserved animal and plant species in Europe.

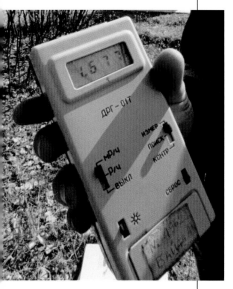

A device to monitor the radiation fallout levels. The Belarus government still makes regular checks of the area to ensure the safety of its people.

## *CHERNOBYL—TWO DECADES LATER*

The explosion at the Chernobyl nuclear power station in 1986 is the most severe nuclear catastrophe in the entire world history of atomic energy use. The explosion sent large clouds of radioactive gases and debris 6 miles (10 km) into the atmosphere. Unfortunately, much of the fallout was blown over Belarus by the wind, and the country is still dealing with the consequences two decades later. The radioactive trace from the explosion affected an estimated 23 percent of Belarus's land, most of it in the southeastern corner of the country near the city of Gomel. The region of Mogilev to the north of Gomel also suffered heavy radiation.

More than 2 million people were directly affected. After the accident, Belarus became an ecological disaster zone.

The impact of the radiation was very uneven, though, with small areas having both clean and contaminated spots. It is estimated that more than 6,000 square miles (15,540 square km) of farmland (20 percent of the total) and the same amount of forest suffered heavy doses of radioactive fallout. Tests have shown that the soil in many other parts of Belarus was affected with low doses of radiation. Many people still grow vegetables on their own allotments, and this food could well be contaminated.

Despite decades of assistance, millions of Belarusians still suffer from radioactive contamination of their food, water, and other resources. Life in the contaminated areas and across Belarus as a whole has been affected by the disaster, with a huge impact on farming and an increase in radiation-related diseases. The two most dangerous radioisotopes, cesium-137 and strontium-90, can still be detected in the soil, water, and dust of the contaminated areas. When strontium is taken internally (ingested through food), it tends to replace calcium in the bones and accumulate radiation, which causes cancer.

Heavy doses of radiation are known to cause several kinds of cancer, although the effects are often delayed for many years, even decades. In the contaminated regions of Belarus, there has been an increase in the number of children contracting leukemia (a cancer of the blood), as well as thyroid cancer, kidney disease, and heart defects. There has also been an increase in the number of children with cancer in the capital, Minsk.

A child born deformed because of the Chernobyl nuclear power plant disaster. In the years following the explosion, there was an increase in malformations of newborn children in Belarus. Many of these children were subsequently abandoned by their parents and left in special-care institutions.

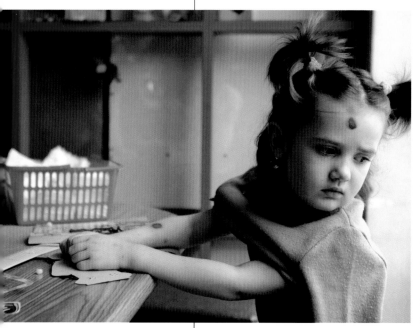

This young girl is receiving treatment for leukemia at the Children's Oncology Center in Minsk. The green-colored marks on her forehead and arms are from medication for an infection.

The government estimates that thyroid cancer among children under the age of 15 rose by 2,000 cases in 1990 and by a further 10,000 cases in 2001. Unofficial estimates suggest that the actual numbers are many times greater. Other types of solid cancers (cancer of organs, rather than of liquids such as blood), which take much longer to become known, could affect many more people in the future.

Scientists and health experts are still unsure about the long-term effects of exposure to low doses of radiation, but this is the greatest worry, since many Belarusians across the whole country were exposed in some degree. These developments are quite frightening for Belarusians, since no one can say how many people will be affected by radiation in the future. The Belarusian people could be feeling the aftereffects of the Chernobyl catastrophe for generations to come.

Leukemia can be treated only with an expensive bone marrow transplant. The Belarus health service is not equipped to offer this kind of treatment. Some sick children have been fortunate enough to be offered medical treatment abroad by international charities, but many more go untreated. International organizations such as the UN have provided some investment in health care and farming projects to improve people's lives, but that alone has not been enough. The Chernobyl Children's Project, for example, spent almost $30 million on health care in the contaminated region, especially in improving local health care to deal with the crisis.

## WILDLIFE AND CHERNOBYL

The most heavily contaminated part of Belarus close to the Chernobyl nuclear reactor has unexpectedly become a haven for local wildlife. Undisturbed by human activity, animals such as wild boar, wisent, roe deer, white-tailed eagles, hawks, elks, and wolves have all prospered in the people-free tranquility of the exclusion zone. Previously the locale of more than 50 state-run farms, humans are now kept out by a barbed-wire fence. There is no traffic, industry, or pesticides being applied in the area. This has had a surprisingly positive impact on local wildlife.

**A wolf and her cub at the Sosnovy Bor National Park in Belarus.**

The Polessky R.eserve was established in the Belarusian part of the exclusion zone in 1988 and now covers an area of 531,300 acres (215,000 ha). There are 16 separate forest ranges inside the reserve, and more than 1,480 acres (600 ha) have been planted with young trees. Unlike nature reserves anywhere else in the world, this one includes special precautions against fire, such as fire breaks, reservoirs, and continuously manned watchtowers. In the last 20 years, the area has become heavily overgrown with grass, bushes, and trees, making it an ideal environment in which wildlife can thrive. For the first time in over 300 years, bears have been spotted in the region.

At the time of the accident, many predicted that the radioactive fallout would wipe out all local animal life, but that has not proved to be the case. Local conservationists have carried out tests on animals living in the radioactive zone to determine if the fallout has caused any ill effects on their health. Their observations have been inconclusive, with some experts believing that the benefits of the exclusion of people from the zone far outweigh any harm to animals from the radiation.

## ENDANGERED ANIMALS

Belarus has 74 mammal species and 221 bird species. The IUCN (International Union for the Conservation of Nature) lists 5 mammal and 4 bird species as critically endangered. These include the wisent, European mink, Eurasian otter, pond bat, and Russian desman (similar to a mole).

Belarus is home to the extremely rare European bison, or wisent. These animals were for a time extinct in Belarus, but were successfully reintroduced into the wild in the early 1920s. They are forest dwellers and are especially numerous in the Belavezhskaya Pushcha National Park. The park stretches across both Belarus and Poland, and wisents live in both countries. Unfortunately, a border security fence stops them from roaming freely throughout the full extent of the forest. Wisents have also made their home in the 20-mile (32-km) exclusion zone around the ruined nuclear reactor at Chernobyl. Since no people now live in this area, the animals have thrived without human interference.

This European mink is critically endangered, mainly because of the thriving fur industry around the world.

## NATIONAL PARKS

Belarus's national parks have become havens for local wildlife and, increasingly, popular tourist destinations for those wanting to see European flora and fauna in an unspoiled setting. Home to some of Europe's oldest primeval forests, Belarus has a number of national parks that have become popular places for fishing and bird-watching. These include the Belavezhskaya Pushcha National Park, Berezinsky Nature Reserve, Narochanski National Park, and the Pripyatski National Park. These venerable forests shelter a number of internationally threatened species, including the wisent.

Narochanski National Park is dominated by its lakes, which harbor many species of fish and other water life. The site of the Berezinsky Nature Reserve is around the Berezina River in the north of the country. It shields more than 50 species of mammals and 217 bird species.

Situated in southwest Belarus, the Belavezhskaya Pushcha National Park is a UNESCO National World Heritage Site and has been classified as a Biosphere Reserve since 1993. The Biosphere Reserve covers an area of 683 square miles (1,771 square km), while the World Heritage Site consists of 338 square miles (876 square km). The park has a relatively mild climate, with temperatures ranging from 25°F to 64°F (−4°C to 18°C), and no more than 50 days of snow per year, making it an ideal environment for numerous plant species. Scotch pine, spruce, hornbeam, small-leaved

*In the 15th century, the Polish king Jogaila used the wild products of the Belavezhskaya forest as a food reserve for his army in preparation for the Battle of Tannenberg.*

lime, oak, sycamore, maple, and birch trees all thrive in the great park. Altogether, more than 900 plant species have been recorded, including 38 nationally threatened species. Typical animals living in the forest include the wisent, wolf, lynx, otter, red deer, and wild boar, among a variety of more than 50 mammal species. Birds include the white stork, peregrine falcon, white-tailed eagle, and eagle owl.

There are fewer than 4,000 people living within the borders of the park, all involved in small-scale farming, mostly growing crops and root vegetables. Those people have very little negative impact on the life of the park. The large amounts of pesticide and fertilizer used by nearby state farms over many years, however, have caused some damage to the reserve. Land reclamation projects, involving the building of waterways and canals to control water levels, have also threatened some of the plant life, especially the Norway spruce.

## INDUSTRIAL POLLUTION

The cities of Belarus are heavily polluted, especially the industrial centers of Navapolatsk and Salihorsk. This is due mainly to heavy industrialization in the 1950s, '60s, and '70s, when Belarus had to be rebuilt and redeveloped following the destruction of World War II. The government recently has recognized this problem but has introduced no broad policies to conserve energy or recycle waste.

Both carbon emissions from motor vehicles and industrial waste from factories affect air quality in Belarus. Automobile exhausts are now the cause of more than half of all pollution in the cities. The average Belarusian creates 1.8 tons (1,633 kg) of carbon waste each year. In the cities, air pollution is on a level with most other industrialized countries.

## WATER RESOURCES

Belarus has over 20,000 rivers and creeks totaling 55,923 miles (90,000 km) in length, as well as 11,000 lakes. Water covers more than 2 percent of the country's total surface. Over half of this water flows into the Black Sea, the remainder into the Baltic Sea. Consequently, Belarus has plenty of water for drinking, farming, and industry, and water shortages have never been a problem in the country. In the decades since World War II, however, pollution from industry and farming has affected many of Belarus's waterways. Water-borne wastes and the misuse of pesticides and fertilizers are the main causes of pollution.

A villager pulling home a barrel of clean water in a village near Minsk.

Little is done to conserve water in Belarus, and Belarusians use a lot of water! Daily consumption of drinking water grew throughout the 1990s and 2000s, and today, water consumption in the Minsk area is higher than in most other European countries. Despite easy access to plentiful supplies of water, 30 percent of samples taken in towns and 50 percent of samples in the country did not measure up to recognized standards of cleanliness.

# BELARUSIANS

THE POPULATION OF BELARUS numbers roughly 9.7 million (2007 estimate). Of these, the majority (81 percent) is ethnic Belarusian. Many Russians have settled in Belarus, particularly during the periods of Russification in the 19th century and in the 20th century as part of the USSR, and are now about 11.5 percent of the population. Other minorities include Poles (4 percent), Ukrainians (2.5 percent), Jews (1 percent), and a small community of Tatar Muslims. The ethnic makeup of Belarus has undergone radical changes during different points in its history. Poles and Jews were once a much larger percentage of the population, and a sizable minority were of German origin.

*Above:* **Belarusian children are dressed warmly for winter activities.**

*Opposite:* **A Belarusian girl wearing the traditional dress of the country.**

The birthrate has changed radically in the years since World War II. Immediately following the war, a baby boom of about 25 births per thousand women flourished, but by the 1960s the birthrate had settled to 14 per thousand. As the population ages, the death rate has increased and the birthrate decreased, so that population figures are currently in decline, with a negative annual growth rate of –0.41 percent. The birthrate is only 1.22 children born per woman, well below the number needed to sustain the population at its current level.

One effect of the nuclear disaster at Chernobyl has been to increase the mortality rate of unborn and newborn babies. The ratio of men to women in the population is also slightly unusual. Many men died during World War II and throughout Stalin's rule in the USSR, leaving a disproportionate number of women who are now entering their retirement years.

A majority of people, up to 72 percent, live in urban areas. There are about 210 major urban areas, with 12 towns of more than 100,000 inhabitants. Population density is quite low with 100 people per square mile (39 per square km). Life expectancy is also low by Western standards—64.63 years for men and 76.4 years for women.

## *BELARUSIANS*

Belarusians are a Slavic people whose ancestors arrived in the area from the north in the sixth century A.D. They are thought to be the descendants of three Slavic tribes—the Krivichi, the Dregovichi, and the Radzimichi—who merged as they settled in the area. Other theories suggest that Belarusians are a mixture of these Slavic tribes with indigenous people from the Baltic region to the northwest. The language spoken in Belarus has some similarity to Baltic languages, which may be a result of this mixture. Among Belarusian academics considerable controversy exists over the origins of Belarusians. But whatever the origins may be, today the people have a very strong sense of ethnic identity.

Some among them, especially those who favor a union with Russia, claim that their early origins do not matter. They see themselves as people who are from the same stock as their neighbors, the Russians.

## RUSSIANS

Russians make up the largest ethnic minority in Belarus. In many of the newly independent Eastern European countries there smolders considerable ethnic hostility among races that had lived together under Communist rule, but this is not the case in Belarus. In the USSR a deliberate policy of Russification meant that Russian families were resettled in large numbers throughout the Soviet Union. In Belarus, the Russification policy was noticeable, with Russian very quickly being adopted as the official language of the country.

Russians within Belarus have their own cultural identity, and there are several cultural organizations that help maintain Russian customs. There also are magazines aimed solely at Russians in the country. In postcommunist Belarus, the Russian Orthodox Church has fared extremely well. Russian families are centered in the urban areas of Belarus and tend to be technical, intellectual, or factory workers rather than farmers.

Employees working in a Minsk refrigerator factory. Many ethnic Russians have factory jobs in Belarus.

*Like Russians, the Ukrainian minority in Belarus folds into the community, using Russian as their language of communication and practicing Orthodox Christianity.*

In recent years
the Lukashenko
government has
come to view the
Polish minority
negatively as
representatives
of pro-Western,
capitalist
Poland. Polish
newspapers have
been forcibly shut
down and local
Polish politicians
silenced.

## POLES

Poles make up about 4 percent of the population, numbering some 400,000 people. They live chiefly in the western region of the country, close to the Polish border. Once a much larger proportion of the population in farming communities and small businesses, large numbers were forcibly deported under Stalin's rule. They have maintained strong ties to neighboring Poland, and their beloved customs distinguish them from Belarusians and Russians. Their religion is Roman Catholicism and services are conducted in the Polish language.

## JEWS

Although they make up only 1 percent of the population of Belarus today, Jews have had a significant effect on the life and culture of the country. Before World War II, Jews dominated business life in Belarus. They were the third-largest ethnic group and were more than 40 percent of the population in cities and towns. The populations of larger cities such as Minsk, Mogilev, Vitebsk, and Gomel were more than 50 percent Jewish. Following the German invasion in June 1941, some 800,000 Belarusian Jews—90 percent of the Jewish population—were killed in the Holocaust. After World War II, many Jews emigrated from Soviet Belarus, and this trend has continued since independence.

The current population figures for Jews are probably wildly inaccurate for several reasons. One is that all citizens of the USSR had to carry internal passports stating their ethnic identity. Many Jews registered as ethnic Belarusians to avoid discrimination. In modern times, many young people are learning for the first time that they are Jewish, now that their parents feel safe enough to tell them about their origins. Many of them are rediscovering their cultural and religious origins, and a religious revival has arisen among young Jews in Belarus. Others are using their Jewish roots as a way to emigrate to Israel, where they may easily become citizens and where they can envision making a better life for themselves.

## OTHERS

About 1 percent of the population of Belarus are people from former Soviet states who were resettled in Belarus, such as Lithuanians and Latvians. One small but culturally discrete group is the Tatars, Muslims from central Asia, who were encouraged to settle in small groups around the former USSR. There is also a small population of Ukrainians.

Jewish youths carrying candles at the site of an old Jewish ghetto called Yama in central Minsk.

## *NATIONAL DRESS*

Dating from the Kievan Rus period (the 13th century), the national dress is not reserved for only special folk festivals in Belarus. Country people still wear traditional dress on fair days and during traditional festivals and other kinds of celebrations. The most distinctive features of Belarusian traditional dress, for both men and women, are the beautifully embroidered linen shirts and blouses. Men's shirts are often embroidered around the collar, sleeves, and across the chest. The pattern of the embroidery differs from region to region, and someone with a little knowledge can tell where a person comes from by the embroidery on his or her clothes. There were once at least a hundred different styles of embroidery in Belarus. In some regions the embroidery is all in red and white, while in others many colors are used.

Both shirts and blouses are long-sleeved. A sleeveless jacket is worn over them; this is usually green or blue and laces up in front. Fancier jackets are embroidered in silver or gold thread, or have silk ribbons sewn onto them.

## WOMEN'S JEWELRY AND HAIRSTYLES

Traditional jewelry for women is fashioned from amber beads or perhaps red coral or silver. Amber is worn in three strands, silver in one strand, and coral in as many as ten, probably a reflection of the prices. In the northwest of the country, silverwork is a well-known craft and typical jewelry has tiny beads mixed with larger, bubblelike spheres. Clasps are often used to fasten the bodice and may be crafted of silver or bronze.

The typical traditional hairstyle for women is two long braids, either left hanging or wound elaborately around the head. In summer flowers would be tucked in. For special occasions, especially weddings, women wear a linen hat shaped like a crown. These are highly ornate, with metal threads sewn into them. More commonly worn is a head shawl with an embroidered section at the front and the ends wound around the face or neck.

Winter skirts are usually woven from wool. Their Belarusian name is *andraki* (and-RAHK-ee). They are often patterned with woven lozenges or stripes in the fabric and are calf- or floor-length. At the waist, women wear a sash knotted at the back with the ends hanging to the hem of the skirt. Over the skirt an apron of fine linen is worn. A pattern of horizontal bars of stars or flowers is woven into this.

Men's clothes are similar, with embroidered shirts, linen trousers for summer and wool for winter, and sleeveless jackets. Outdoor clothes for both men and women consist of sheepskin jackets embroidered with wool, felt boots, and hooded garments made of thick cloth. Outer coats are usually white with red embroidery in the Gomel region and deep blue cord in the Bykhov region, while in other regions green cord or black leather is common. Men's waistbands are woven in herringbone or diamond designs. They are tied at the side and the tails hang to the knee. Men's hats are cone-shaped and are called *magerki* (mag-ERK-ee). They are usually made of felt, but some are made of sheepskin.

Irving Berlin (1888–1989) emigrated with his family to New York in 1893. He became an important composer in the United States and wrote the scores for many famous Broadway and movie musicals. He also gave us "God Bless America."

## SOME FAMOUS BELARUSIANS

In Belarus, notable personages include ancient scholars such as Saint Efrosinia of Polotsk, a 12th-century religious leader; Francis Skaryna, who was the first person to print the Bible in Belarusian, around 1517; and Symon Budny, a 16th-century writer in the Belarusian language. Budny had radical ideas for his time. He strongly criticized church clergy who made no effort to explain religion to the common people. He was a priest himself in the Calvinist church for a while, but was ejected from the community after publishing his most important work, which was concerned with religion, politics, and the rights of the individual.

One of the most infamous Belarusians was Felix Dzerzhinsky (1877–1926), a Communist contemporary of Lenin's. In 1917 he became head of the Soviet secret police, the Cheka, the forerunner of the KGB. Dzerzhinsky was responsible for the imprisonment and death of tens of thousands of Soviet citizens in his zeal to obliterate enemies of the Communist revolution. Today, a statue of Dzershinsky stands outside the KGB headquarters in Minsk. In the Soviet era, towns and factories throughout the USSR were named after him.

Many famous people came originally from Belarus. Numerous Jews, in particular, have left Belarus for the United States or Israel to start new lives. Marc Chagall (1887–1985), the artist, lived in Belarus until his early adulthood. He was born in Vitebsk when it was a part of Russia. When it became part of the Belorussian Soviet Socialist Republic, Chagall enthusiastically took a leading role in the new regime, but he grew disillusioned and left the country soon after, never to return. Menachem Begin (1913–92), a former prime minister of Israel, was also born in Belarus. During World War II he lost his family but managed to escape to Israel.

A famous American composer, Irving Berlin (1888–1989), was born in Mogilev but emigrated with his family to the United States. He wrote countless popular songs,

Vitaly Scherbo is a famous Belarusian gymnast, winning six gold medals in the 1992 Summer Olympics in Barcelona, Spain.

including "White Christmas," "Puttin' on the Ritz," and "There's No Business Like Show Business," as well as the scores for musicals such as *Easter Parade* and *White Christmas*. Sir Isaac Schoenberg played a very important role in the history of television. He invented the world's first high-definition television system. He was born in Pinsk in 1880 and lived in the USSR until 1914 when he emigrated to England.

Belarus today has several famous sports personalities. Minsk native Vitaly Scherbo, a six-time gold medalist in Olympic gymnastics, represented Belarus in the Atlanta Olympics in 1996. The gymnast Olga Korbut grew up in Belarus and represented the USSR in the Olympics in 1972 and 1976. She won three gold medals and a silver medal in the 1972 Olympics where she became the first person to achieve a backward somersault on the uneven parallel bars. Belarus won 19 medals in the 2008 Summer Olympics in Beijing, China.

# LIFESTYLE

SINCE INDEPENDENCE IN 1991, the lives of the people of Belarus have undergone the most radical changes imaginable. They have taken part in the dismantling of one of the most powerful empires in history; they have suffered the economic upheaval resulting from becoming a part of the world economy and dealing with a free market; they have seen the sureties of their lives, such as guaranteed employment for life and free health care, gradually give way to food shortages, closed factories, and rationing; and, most harrowing of all, they have lived with, and continue to deal with, the lethal consequences of Chernobyl, the worst nuclear accident in history.

Amid these upheavals, the people of Belarus are getting on with their daily lives while making decisions about their country's future that may either lead them back to union with Russia or to a future of independence and closer ties with the West.

*Left:* **Outside the cities and suburbs, people live in their own single-story homes.**

*Opposite:* **Busy urban Belarusians walking from where they had just gotten off a city bus.**

**Belarusians walking in an underground passage in the modern city of Minsk.**

# LIFE IN THE CITIES

Belarusians spend the days of their lives in the same way as millions of other Europeans. The majority of people live in cities and travel to work each day in efficient mass-transportation systems.

Minsk, the capital, is a modern city that was almost completely rebuilt from the ruins left by World War II. The city center has long, wide, straight roads lined with comparatively small apartment and office buildings. Most citizens live in the suburbs in multistory housing developments. Modern amenities such as nursery schools, shopping centers, and movie theaters are close by, and buildings are surrounded gracefully by trees and parks rather than major highways. These 75-acre (30-ha) developments have names such as Vostok 1 (named after the first human spaceflight, by cosmonaut Yuri Gagarin, in 1961) and Vostok 2, and house anywhere from 15,000 to 50,000 residents.

From 1971 to 1975, 47 million square feet (4.4 million square m) of housing was built. Most housing is owned by the government and rents have been kept artificially low so that housing costs are usually no more than 7 percent of the average family budget. Some people have built their own homes with government subsidies.

## OTHER CITIES IN BELARUS

While Minsk is a thriving, modern industrial and cultural center, other cities in Belarus have different atmospheres and distinct cultural and social lives.

After Minsk, Brest is the most vibrant city in Belarus. It is near the border with Poland, and for many years was a part of Poland. Brest has all the bustling atmosphere of a border town with both Poles and Belarusians making use of the border crossing for quick shopping trips. The city has become the focal point for the smuggling of contraband goods between Russia and Western Europe.

Grodno, in the west of the country, is very close to Lithuania and, having suffered less havoc in World War II, has many more intact historical buildings than Minsk.

Vitebsk, in the north of the country, also has a historic atmosphere. It is an ancient town that acquired some of its history while it was part of Russia.

Polotsk has a different ambience altogether. Compared with the prosperous industrial might of Minsk and the cultural heritage of Vitebsk, it seems to be a sleepy river town. Yet it was once the most important city in Belarus and at various times has been part of Lithuania, Poland, and Russia. Its many historical buildings have survived because the town has endured less industrial development than other sites in the region.

Today, many of the people in Minsk work in the manufacturing sector, building tractors, television sets, motorcycles, electrical items, and other factory goods. Like the city buildings, many of the factories also were built in the wake of World War II. Although car ownership is increasing, many residents travel to and from work on public transportation, either by streetcar or bus.

There are about 6 million cell phones in Belarus. Only a small number of people are connected to the Internet, and most of this group are young and often are university graduates. Homes are small but quite modern with sound and heat insulation. Town dwellers largely live in small family units. Married couples sometimes live with their parents while waiting for their own apartment. Housing became a huge problem after the Chernobyl disaster when thousands of people had to be relocated around the cities in specially built complexes. As a result, hopeful residents sometimes have to wait a long while for an apartment to become available.

## *LIFE IN THE COUNTRY*

In the country, life is somewhat slower and more relaxed than in the fast-paced cities. The small family-owned farms that once dominated the countryside of Belarus have long given way to collective farms, and people live in small village communities in separate houses.

While newer houses are made with brick or prefabricated units, there are still many traditional wooden houses. Those were once built by a whole village community as they were needed, each in the same style. A wooden shingle or thatched roof covered a one-story building of two rooms. Built onto it was a lean-to, used as a storage room or a cooler place to sleep during hot summer nights.

Inside a country house, furniture consists of plain wooden planks placed around the walls as benches. These often serve as beds with simple mattresses made of feathers or straw thrown on. In traditional houses, embroidered linen cloths decorate the walls. A simple staircase leads up to an attic where cured (preserved and flavored) food is stored. Older houses also have a cellar.

## THE DECLINE OF RURAL COMMUNITIES

As the gradual industrialization of Belarus has brought about migrations to the cities, village life has declined to the point where in many places entire villages stand desolate and crumbling. This has imposed a negative effect on the survival of the culture of Belarus because it is in the rural areas where age-old traditions cling to life. As villages slowly fade away, many traditions are disappearing, too.

In addition to the gradual migration of rural families to the cities, the remaining country folk are also having smaller families, leading to even fewer people in the vanishing villages.

Rural houses often have a garden with fruit trees, a shed for gardening tools, and a vegetable plot. In addition, a family will often have chickens and perhaps goats or a pig being fattened for market. When farms were smaller, the sheds would have held the plows and horses and might also have been a space for curing and smoking food, as well as a threshing room. Nowadays, the main business of farms is carried out in huge factory-like buildings where the harvested food is partly processed before being sent to markets or factories.

In the villages, schools are small and rustic in nature. They often include a small farm, a fishpond, or a museum.

The communal bathhouse is another feature of rural life. Called a *banya* (BAN-yah), the bathhouse may be owned by a single family or shared by neighbors. It is much like a sauna, built of wood and standing in the open near a lake or river. Inside is a woodstove. Water scented with mint leaves or juice from birch trees is poured onto the hot stove, creating a fragrant, steam-filled atmosphere. A good steaming in the sauna is followed by a roll in the snow or a quick dip into the frigid river or lake.

*Houses in the same village may have similar patterns carved on the gables of their roofs. In one area, for example, all the gables have a carving of the sun surrounded by foliage.*

Women working in a fish packing factory. Unfortunately, women generally receive lesser wages than men.

*An all-women's political party opposed to the Lukashenko regime, the Belarusian Women's Party "Nadzieja," was created in 1994 to support women's issues. In 2007 the party was shut down by the Belarusian government for purported administrative irregularities.*

## WOMEN AND THE FAMILY

Nuclear families are the norm in Belarus, and a high proportion of people choose marriage over cohabitation or living alone. Children are considered important to the family, if not the single most important reason for marrying. Women have had economic equality in Belarus for many years. In most cases this means that a much higher burden falls on the women's shoulders, as they take on responsibility both for their children and their jobs. In the majority of families, two parents' incomes are essential for survival rather than career moves for the mothers.

Since women usually work in low-paid industries, their wages in general are about one-third lower than men's.

Belarus has one of the highest divorce rates in the world, with three out of every seven marriages ending in divorce. Many Belarusians attribute this to the greater hardship of living in the postcommunist world, with husbands often not earning very much and women having few opportunities to develop careers and get good jobs. Unlike policies in many other European countries, families receive very little help from the state.

## EDUCATION

Education is compulsory in Belarus between the ages of 6 and 15. Preschool education is subsidized by the state, and most children attend nursery school. Primary education lasts from age 6 to 10, while "basic" education spans ages 10 to 15, up to the ninth grade. School costs and textbooks are paid for by the state. Teaching is largely in Russian, although Belarusian has been reinstated.

At the age of 15, students can end their education, continue with academic studies, or change to a vocational or specialist school of some kind. Children with particular aptitudes can attend schools dedicated to music, foreign languages, mathematics, science, or sports. There are about 250 vocational and technical schools in Belarus. Vocational schools include schools of car maintenance, construction, teacher training, machine building, radio technology, and many others. Sports schools are very important in Belarus with 64 in Minsk alone. Some of these schools specialize in one discipline, such as ice hockey, horse riding, fencing, and gymnastics. At the top of the system are 44 state higher education colleges and a number of universities for undergraduate and postgraduate studies.

The National Library of Belarus in Minsk. Located in a unique building, this library circulates an impressive range of books and digital media, aimed at increasing the educational level of the people.

**A bride and groom pose for a photograph with their families.**

# *MARRIAGE*

In modern-day Belarus, wedding celebrations resemble those in many Western countries, although some rural villages still observe a few traditional customs. For instance, marriages in villages are sometimes arranged by the parents, though only with the agreement of their children. The couple usually becomes formally engaged with the approval of their parents and the exchange of rings. In small villages, the bride-to-be will travel around the village to invite everyone to the wedding, but in towns and cities, wedding invitations are mailed. In rural areas, people still prepare a special bread for the wedding day that is large, round, and ornately decorated with pinecones.

Today all couples must marry at the local registry office, but many couples also take part in a ceremony at their church or synagogue (the place of worship for a Jewish congregation). So after the registry office formalities, the wedding party moves on to the church for the religious service. The bride wears a white or pink dress, though in some areas the dress is traditionally blue. She wears flowers in her hair and is often attended by bridesmaids. The groom and his party wear white and blue flowers, while the bride and her party wear white and pink flowers.

After the couple has exchanged their marriage vows, everyone is invited to the bride's home or to a restaurant for a celebratory meal. The bride and groom cut the wedding cake at this gathering. Guests bring gifts of cash, embroidery, or some useful household object.

Many weddings in the cities and towns take two days: one day for the official wedding at the registry office and the second day for the religious service in a church and celebratory party.

## CHILDREN

When a baby is about two months old, Orthodox Christian Belarusians hold a christening ceremony, giving the child a Christian name through baptism, in which godparents, people who sponsor the godchild at its baptism, are chosen. Guests present gifts, and a party is held at the family home.

Traditionally, the new grandmother was driven around to friends to announce the happy news of the christening. Men fired guns into the air, and, later, the grandmother served guests *babina kasha* (bah-BEE-nah KAH-sha), the traditional old lady's porridge.

**Children enjoying an exercise break in a park in Minsk.**

77

## *LIFE AFTER CHERNOBYL*

It is easy, more than two decades after the nuclear catastrophe at Chernobyl, to assume that the danger has faded, but for the thousands of people still living within the contaminated zone in southern Belarus, radiation will continue to be a prominent health hazard into the foreseeable future.

Immediately after the accident, thousands of people were evacuated from the area and new housing developments were hastily built to accommodate them. But this was at a time when the economy was failing and industries could not provide sufficient jobs in the newly settled areas. Many chose therefore to return to their contaminated land, while at the same time people from other areas migrated there to occupy the empty houses, farm the land, and gather fruits and berries from the forest.

The chief peril for people in these contaminated zones is in the soil rather than the air. Radiation is transferred from the soil to plants and, if the soil is turned while plowing, is released into the air. In the years

**A solemn gathering of people in Minsk to commemorate the victims of Chernobyl.**

following the explosion, this sequence was not widely understood, so farming in the region continued and crops that contained unsafe levels of radiation were sold all over the country. Some collective farms continued to produce food even after the soil had been declared unsafe and food production banned. Such forest products as mushrooms and berries are particularly susceptible to contamination. When they are harvested and sold in the markets, they spread the contamination around the whole country. Dust storms and the wheels of vehicles crossing the area also carry the contamination throughout Belarus.

In recent years, the government has increased investment in the contaminated zone by offering funding to farmers to continue working the land, which otherwise would be abandoned. Government inspectors regularly carry out tests on locally grown vegetables to make sure they do not contain dangerous levels of radiation. There have been increasing health problems among those living in the contaminated zone, however, with cancer being a common disease—especially in children.

## HEALTH

Like education, health care is free in Belarus, although it has become severely strained because of increased health problems after the nuclear accident at Chernobyl. Since independence, the quality of medical care in Belarus (and in much of the former Soviet Union) has declined, with essential medicines often not easily available. Since the early 1990s, immunizations against basic diseases have fallen and the number of infant deaths has risen. There has been a massive rise among children in the number of thyroid cancers, a long-term illness. One estimate suggests that the number of cases could rise to 10,000 with a possible 1,000 deaths. Sadly, there has been a general downslide in the overall health of children. At present the infant mortality rate in Belarus is twice that of the United States. AIDS has also become a serious problem in Belarus, partly due to a home-grown drug that is injected with unsterilized needles.

# RELIGION

ACCORDING TO ITS CONSTITUTION, Belarus has no official religion. For 70 years or so, from the establishment of the USSR in 1922 to independence in 1991, Belarus was an atheist country officially. All religions were severely restricted, and many leading church figures fled abroad to set up communities in England, the United States, and Western Europe. Nonetheless, since independence, there has been a vigorous revival in religious belief and worship as young people seek their religious roots, hoping to find spiritual aspects to their lives that they felt were lacking under a Communist regime. But religion and politics are

*Above:* **Candles are lit during a church service in a cathedral in Minsk.**

*Opposite:* **A picture of Christ adorns this hand-painted wooden box.**

inextricably mixed. The religious groups that have undergone a revival in Belarus have a political as well as a religious agenda for the country.

There are two main branches of Christianity in Belarus: the Orthodox Church and the Roman Catholic Church. Some Protestant Christian groups are present and also small Jewish and Muslim communities. Large numbers of people remain atheistic or uncommitted.

## EARLY RELIGIONS

The earliest religions in Belarus were non-Christian. Before A.D. 990, Slavic tribes, called the Krivichi, worshiped their sun god, Yaryla. Their religion was Druidic in nature and revolved around the seasons. Tribal rituals in spring summoned the beginning of the new season, while in April and October the dead were commemorated with food and drinks taken to the graves. Kaliady, a celebration of the winter solstice, is still celebrated in Belarus.

Religious artifacts from the early period include stone obelisks—rectangular pillars tapering toward a pyramidal top—used in sacrifices. Figures carved out of stone have also been found.

## THE ORTHODOX CHURCH

Christianity came to Belarus from Greece in A.D. 990 in the form of Eastern Orthodoxy. This mode of Christianity historically accepts church leadership from Constantinople (modern Istanbul) rather than the Vatican in Rome. It differs from the Roman Catholic Church in some of its beliefs and rituals. Several religious figures, including Saint Efrosinia of Polotsk and Simeon Polotsky, were very influential in the Church's history.

Eastern Orthodoxy became the official religion of Greater Lithuania when it was embraced by the rulers of Kievan Rus. As the centuries passed and power passed from Lithuanian to Polish hands, Orthodoxy staunchly remained the religion of the peasants of Belarus. In the 1920s the religion was swept away in the reforms of the Russian Revolution, but it has seen a revival in recent years.

The Eastern Orthodox Church affirms seven mysteries or sacraments: baptism (christening), confirmation (anointing with holy oil), communion, taking holy orders, penance, anointing of the sick, and marriage. Unlike the Catholic Church, where children are baptized but not given communion until about age 7, the Eastern faith baptizes and confirms each child in the faith at the same time so that they can take part in communion.

The Orthodox marriage ceremony symbolizes an eternal union between husband and wife. Remarriage after divorce is possible in Eastern Orthodoxy, but only on the understanding that the original union was not entered into effectively and that the vows were not taken seriously.

Fasting is important in Eastern Orthodoxy, practiced much more zealously than in other branches of Christianity. Fasting takes place on several occasions: Lent, the Fast of the Apostles in June, the Assumption in August, and Advent in the period before Christmas. Fasting rules include giving up meat and animal products as well as wine and oil.

Prayer is a public activity in the Orthodox Church. While private prayer is also part of the religion, the silent prayers are the same as those recited aloud in church and in monasteries. It is this sense of a community of worshipers rather than lone individuals that distinguishes the beliefs of this church from Catholicism.

A bishop is either unmarried or widowed, but the priests and deacons (a cleric ranking just below a priest in Christian churches; one of the Holy Orders) are allowed to marry, unlike in the Catholic Church.

There are about 800 Orthodox congregations, and Belarus has been designated an exarchate of the Russian Orthodox Church, meaning that it is a new branch of the church with its own bishop. In 1990, 60 percent of the population considered themselves to be active Orthodox Christians. By 2007 this figure had shrunk to 47 percent. There are now a seminary for training priests, three convents, and a monastery in Belarus.

*Above and opposite:* **Two Orthodox churches—a traditional one in Vitebsk that is made mostly of wood** *(above)*, **and the striking onion-shaped domes of a church in Brest** *(opposite)*.

## *ROMAN CATHOLICISM*

Roman Catholicism became a significant religion in Belarus during the time when Belarus was part of Greater Lithuania. Greater Lithuania formed a union in the 14th century with Poland, a firmly Roman Catholic country. As a result of that union, a strong Roman Catholic influence appeared in Belarus, largely through the Polish-speaking people in the west of the country. Many of the aristocrats were Roman Catholics, while the peasants were mostly Eastern Orthodox.

The Roman Catholic Church accepts the pope as its temporal leader. All priests take a vow of celibacy, and women are not admitted into the priesthood. Divorce, contraception, and abortion are all forbidden by the church. Prayer is mostly a private communication between an individual and God.

About 20 percent of the population of Belarus is Roman Catholic: a quarter of this group are ethnic Poles, while three-quarters are Belarusian. There is some conflict within the Catholic Church in Belarus over the language of the Mass. Most Catholic services are conducted in Polish, although Pope John Paul II (1920–2005) himself had conducted services in Belarusian. There are more than 80 Catholic priests in Belarus, every one of them Polish in origin. The Roman Catholic Church in Belarus is headed by an ethnic Pole, Archbishop Tadeusz Kondrusiewicz (b. 1946).

## THE UNIATE CHURCH

The presence of both Eastern Orthodoxy and Roman Catholicism has resulted in severe conflict between the two churches. In the 16th century, the aristocracy of Belarus was predominantly Polish and Catholic, while the peasants remained loyal to Eastern Orthodoxy. In 1595 an attempt was made through the Treaty of Brest to resolve the disparity by creating the Uniate Church (a church in Eastern Europe or the Middle East that acknowledges papal authority but retains its own liturgy). It used Belarusian as the language of services and adopted Orthodox doctrine but acknowledged the Roman Catholic pope as the head of the church. It met with scant success among the mass of the population and became the pliable tool of various political groups until it was banned altogether in 1839. Since 1990, unsuccessful attempts have been made to reestablish that church, which has many branches outside Belarus, including the United States, Canada, and Australia.

*Opposite:* **A congregation arriving at a Roman Catholic church in Grodno.**

*A branch of the Uniate Church exists in Toronto, Canada. In 1992 the prelate of the Toronto Uniate Church, Archbishop Mikalaj, visited the Uniate Church community in Minsk.*

### RELIGION AND LANGUAGE

In a country where choosing a language to speak is a contentious issue, the newly flowering churches have also become embroiled in political issues. The Roman Catholic Church is considered to be essentially Polish, although the majority of Catholics now are ethnic Belarusian. Most Catholic services are conducted in Polish, and Polish flags hang in many Catholic churches. Large numbers of ethnic Belarusians live in Bielastok inside Poland and are Orthodox Christians. Some claim that they are discriminated against in a region that Belarusian politicians have described as more Belarusian in character than Polish.

Meanwhile, in Orthodox churches, services are conducted in Russian and the regional head for Belarus is a Russian, Metropolitan Filaret. For many Belarusians with strong nationalist feelings, this arrangement is unsatisfactory. To remedy the situation, Metropolitan Filaret has commissioned a translation of the Bible into modern Belarusian and has included Belarusian festivals on the religious calendar.

**This statue of Francis Skaryna, a famous 16th century humanist, stands in his birthplace of Polotsk.**

## *IMPORTANT CHURCH FIGURES*

**SAINT EFROSINIA OF POLOTSK** (1110–67) Saint Efrosinia was the granddaughter of Prince Useslau, the Magician of Polotsk. She felt she had a vocation from an early age and, refusing all offers of marriage, ran off to her aunt's convent. She later founded her own convent and was joined by other female members of her family. Moreover, she founded a monastery for monks and was the abbess (the superior of a group of nuns) of both the institutions. One of her occupations was to hand make copies of religious works, which she sold to earn alms for the poor. She died in 1167 during a pilgrimage to the Holy Land in Jerusalem and her remains were carried back to Kiev, Ukraine, where they were buried in the Monastery of the Caves. Those relics were finally returned to Polotsk in 1910. The Church of the Holy Savior, which she had built, still stands in Polotsk. She figures importantly today in the Eastern Orthodox Church.

**FRANCIS SKARYNA** Born probably in 1490 in Polotsk, Francis Skaryna translated and published the first Bible written in the Belarusian language. He was a humanist rather than a religious leader, although his translation made the Bible's content available to the peasants of Belarus for the first time. He was an important figure in the Renaissance, with wide interests in theology, botany, poetry, law, art, and medicine. In 1530, after a fire destroyed his printing presses, Skaryna went to Prussia, where he served as the doctor to Albreicht, the Duke of Prussia, for a while. In his later years he became a gardener to Ferdinand Hapsburg, the king of Bohemia.

## OTHER RELIGIONS IN BELARUS

**JUDAISM** Jewish communities have existed in Belarus since the 14th century. By 1914 Jews made up about 14 percent of the population, living largely in the cities. They constituted fully 50 percent of the residents in some places. As a result of the genocide of World War II and consequent emigration, Jews now count for only around 1 percent of the population.

The rabbi is the spiritual leader of a Jewish community. Worship in the home is just as important as in the synagogue, and the religion lays down strict rules about its practice. The Jewish Sabbath (a day of rest and worship) is from Friday evening to Saturday evening.

One branch of Judaism, the Chabad-Lubavitch movement, about 250,000 strong, was founded in Belarus by Rabbi Schneur Zalmon in 1798. It runs 1,300 Hebrew schools and other institutions around the world.

Since independence, there has been a flowering of Judaism in Belarus. Although Jewish people are still emigrating to Israel, others are rediscovering their roots and the venerable customs of their religion. There is a yeshiva, an academy or seminary for the advanced study of Jewish texts, in Belarus, and many Jewish Sunday schools are being opened to teach Hebrew and the Talmud. About 70 Jewish organizations are active in Belarus. Because of the steady emigration of Belarusian Jews to Israel since independence, however, some estimates suggest that if the current trend continues, there will be no Jewish community remaining in Belarus within 20 years.

**ISLAM** There is a small number of Muslims living in Belarus, mostly Tatars who settled there in the 11th century. Some of the first Belarusian texts were actually written phonetically in Arabic by Muslim imams (prayer leaders). Like other religions in Belarus, Islam also suffered suppression during the Soviet years. Today, there are active mosques in the towns of Navahrudak, Slonim, and Smilovichi, and a new mosque is planned for the capital, Minsk.

*Along with Eastern Orthodoxy and Roman Catholicism, small groups of Protestants practice their religion in Belarus. There are altogether about 200 Baptist churches and 350 other Protestant congregations.*

# LANGUAGE

WHEN THE NEWSPAPER *Zviadia* greeted its readers on New Year's Day in 1992, its message was printed in five languages: Belarusian, Russian, Polish, Yiddish, and Ukrainian. Except for the last, all these languages were in official use in the liberal early years under the Soviet Union.

Today, the Russian language is dominant. While Belarus was part of the Russian Empire, and when it was part of the USSR, the Belarusian language was discouraged and finally banned outright. The language has suffered greatly as a result. It is still in use, but it is an endangered language and only 11 percent of the population, mostly those living in rural areas, speak it fluently. Nonetheless, as many as 80 percent of Belarusians consider Belarusian as their mother tongue, even though they speak it imperfectly.

*Above:* **Posters placed along Frantsisk Skorina (Francis Skaryna) Avenue in Minsk.**

*Opposite:* **Old friends sharing a laugh in the Palesse region of Belarus.**

The first signs of perestroika, or reform, in Belarus came in 1986 when a group of intellectuals wrote to Mikhail Gorbachev, the leader of the USSR, asking for the country's language to be recognized. In 1990, shortly before independence, Belarusian was declared the national language, and an incubation period of 10 years was decided on until it would become the main language to be used officially in public life. Street signs were changed to Belarusian. Today, both languages (Russian and Belarusian) are used in schools.

Yiddish, spoken by the Jewish community, has become a minority language since World War II and the Stalinist era. Only a few still speak it at home. Polish is also a minority language and is spoken primarily in Roman Catholic Church services. The language of the Tatars is of Turkic

**The University of Polotsk. It was closed down temporarily in 1864 when the Russian Empire banned the Belarusian language.**

ancestry, and although the number of Tatar people in Belarus is small, the language is still spoken in isolated pockets. Since the breakup of the Soviet central government, many Tatar people, forcibly relocated by the Soviets throughout the former USSR, have seized the opportunity to return to the Crimea (a Ukrainian peninsula between the Black Sea and the Sea of Azov), their former home.

## *EARLY ROOTS OF LANGUAGE*

By the 13th century, the language used in the Grand Duchy of Lithuania was the Belarusian language. It was used in all official matters and was spoken by most of the population. In 1569 the Treaty of Lublin merged Lithuania with Poland and a gradual process of "Polonization" began. Polish became the language of the court and the Catholic Church, while the peasantry continued to speak Belarusian.

Between the 14th and 16th centuries the written form of Belarusian developed, using the Cyrillic alphabet. The scholar Francis Skaryna published works in Belarusian, notably the Bible, followed by Symon Budny, Simeon Polotsky, and many others. Belarusian became the dynamic force in the emerging printing trades, and its translations from Latin were used to produce Russian and Polish texts.

In the 18th century, the region of Belarus was incorporated into the Russian Empire and the process of Russification began. The Belarusian language was suppressed, and Russian became the language of the courts, administration, and church. In 1864 all Belarusian publications were banned, schools were closed, and the University of Polotsk was shut down. Belarusian became the language of the illiterate peasants, while education, social mobility, and a career required Russian.

The fortunes of the Belarusian language improved after the Belorussian Soviet Socialist Republic was declared to be under Soviet rule in 1919. Dissidents returned from Europe and began writing in their native language, schools and universities were reopened, and teaching and publishing again took place in Belarusian.

But by the late 1920s, the honeymoon period of tolerance was over and the process of Russification set in again. Teacher training was in Russian, so new teachers taught only in that language. As older Belarusian teachers retired and died, the language disappeared with them. By the late 1980s, there was not a single school in the capital, Minsk, using any Belarusian. Russian had become the language of commerce, education, government, even conversation in factories. While illiteracy was virtually eradicated and educational standards grew as quickly as did economic security, it was at the expense of the Belarusian language.

Then, in 1990, amid an upsurge of nationalist feeling just before independence, Belarusian was declared the national language. Street signs were changed back to Belarusian, and the language was reintroduced into classrooms. But for many people this was going too far too fast. After all, Russian was the most commonly spoken language. Many parents were reluctant to see their children educated in a minority language that no one outside Belarus could understand. Consequently, in 1995 a referendum established both Russian and Belarusian as national languages.

*The first written use of the Belarusian language was in early Tatar religious texts, using Arabic letters but Belarusian words.*

## *BELARUSIAN*

Belarusian is an east Slavic language, closely related to both Russian and Ukrainian. The Slavs who first moved into the area spread around the Eastern Europe region carrying their language with them. As they settled, their language merged with the indigenous languages they encountered. There are now around 11 Slavic languages divided into three groups. Russian, Belarusian, and Ukrainian are all in the same group and have many common words.

Belarusian, like Russian, is written in the Cyrillic alphabet. That alphabet originated in the ninth century when the Greek missionary brothers Cyril and Methodius adapted the Greek alphabet to produce the scriptures in Slavic languages. Originally the alphabet had 43 characters, but the many languages that make use of the Cyrillic alphabet have each fine-tuned it to their own needs, so that alphabets may vary. Belarusian can also be written in a Roman form, but this is rarely used, since no one agrees on a spelling system.

## THE POLITICS OF LANGUAGE

Since independence, Belarus and Russia have considered a political union of the two countries.

Language has become a part of more complex issues, such as choosing between an independent Belarus and one closely tied to Russia. Many intellectuals believe that the Belarusian culture is enshrined in the language and that if the language dies, there will no longer be a Belarus and the place will simply become another region of Russia.

For other people the issue is simpler. They have been learning Russian all their lives and see it as a means of advancement beyond the borders of Belarus. They feel that there is little point in retaining a language that no one really uses fluently, especially when they already have Russian, which works well both inside and outside of the country.

Many Belarusian words are Russian words with slightly different spellings and pronunciations. Belarusian has also borrowed from Polish, a quite unrelated Slavic language. In other ways, Belarusian is closer to Ukrainian. Both of these languages have a vowel pronounced "ee" while there is no such sound in Russian. Belarusian also has a unique letter pronounced like the English "w" as in "wait."

Of several regional dialects of Belarusian, the most unusual is the one spoken in Pinsk. People from Pinsk call themselves Pinchuki (pin-CHOOK-ee), after the area where they live, and speak a dialect that has many words and expressions not found in standard Belarusian. They

This cafe's signboard shows its name written in the Cyrillic alphabet.

consider theirs to be a language different from Belarusian, and many believe the Pinsk language and culture to have origins separate from the rest of Belarus.

Often encyclopedias and other references have different spellings for the same name or place in Belarus. Many of these variations result from one book using a Russian form of the word while another uses the Belarusian form. For example, the town sometimes shown as Grodno is often spelled as Hrodno. Similarly, Gomel may be spelled Homel. This is because in Russian the Cyrillic character is pronounced as a hard *g* while the same character in Belarusian is pronounced as *h*. President Lukashenko's name is spelled as Lukashenka when transliterated using the Belarusian pronunciation. Even "Belarus" can be spelled many different ways!

## *RUSSIAN*

Russian is the most widely spoken language in Belarus. Like Belarusian, it uses the Cyrillic alphabet, although some of its characters are different. It has 33 characters and several of its sounds are completely unfamiliar to English speakers.

In many cases several English characters have to be used to represent one single Russian sound. For example, the Russian word for cabbage stew has two letters—Щ И—but must be represented in English by six letters—*shchee*.

After years of Russification a new pidgin language has evolved in Belarus that is a mixture of Belarusian and Russian grammar and vocabulary. This language is called *trasyanka* (traz-YAN-kah) and is spoken by at least half the population in varying degrees. It functions as a "street Russian" spoken by people who have adopted Russian without learning the academic rules of the language.

## WHAT'S IN A NAME?

If you have read other books or perhaps encyclopedias about Belarus, you will have noticed that there are many spellings of the country's name. Bielorussia, Byelorussia, Belorussia (White Russia), and Belarus are a few of the ways to write it in English.

The literal translation, "White Russia," comes from the ancient term Belaya Rus. This term was first used in the 16th century by an English writer, Sir Jerome Horsey. Many suggestions have been made for the origin of the word *belaya* or "white." Czarist Russia reasserted this term to separate Belarus from its Polish-Lithuanian heritage, after Belarus became a part of Imperial Russia in the 19th century. It might refer to the beauty of the countryside or the vast white blanket of snow in winter. One suggestion is that the word white means "free" and was used for the part of Belarus that was not invaded by the Tatars. The word Rus comes from the area of land formed by a triangle of three cities: Kiev, Chernigov, and Pereyaslaval (all in modern Ukraine). It is probably the same root word as in "Russia," and was used to refer to all Orthodox Christians. As the Tatars (who were Muslims) took over the Ukraine, the center of Christian Orthodoxy became Moscow and so the name, Rus, moved with the religion.

While Belarus was part of the USSR, the official spelling in English was Byelorussia. After independence it was called, in Belarusian, Respublika Bielarus, which was morphed into Belarus by the Western media. Nationalists prefer the spelling Belarus since it distances the nation from Russia. Those in favor of union with Russia prefer the older spelling.

People enthusiastically examining books at a book fair in Belarus.

95

# ARTS

OVER THE CENTURIES Belarusian culture and arts have flourished and declined in turn. The Renaissance saw a flourishing of architecture and literature, while the 19th and early 20th century were also good times for Belarusian culture. Belarusian émigrés have also contributed to the arts in their new homes in many lands.

During the Soviet era the socialist realism school of art and architecture was popular. Traditional crafts, folk songs, folk dances, and music of all kinds survived the various upheavals and misfortunes that have occurred throughout Belarus's history, and poetry and theater have remained important aspects of the life of the country. Yiddish literature also prospered in Belarus, and many famous Jewish figures in the American media and arts had their beginnings in this little-known backwater of the Russian Empire. Marc Chagall, a particularly well-known artist who was originally from Belarus, used his hometown as a theme in many of his paintings.

*Below:* **An impressive sculpture stands in front of an apartment house in Minsk. Historical and domestic subjects were a common theme in much of Belarusian art.**

*Opposite:* **Doll-like wooden chess pieces in a set in Minsk.**

## MARC CHAGALL

Vitebsk's most famous citizen must be Marc Chagall. He was born in 1887 when Vitebsk was part of the Russian Empire. He came from a modest Jewish family of eight children and went to a Jewish primary school and a Russian language secondary school. He studied art under a local realist artist, Yehuda Pen, and then went to Saint Petersburg to study more formally.

Chagall painted his early works before the period of the surrealist school of art, but they are very much in a surreal style. He abandoned realist rules about logic in pictures, painting instead a reality more psychological than representative. He spent some years in Europe studying with other bohemian artists and poets and, under their encouraging influence, developed his whimsical style. Many of his paintings were images recalled from his home life in Vitebsk. He returned to Vitebsk in 1914 and married a local Jewish girl named Bella Rosenfeld. He started painting in a realist style again, and his wife appears in many of his paintings.

Chagall enthusiastically joined in the October Revolution in 1917 and became the commissar (political officer) for art at the local academy and museum. But gradually he became disillusioned with the revolution and left both Russia and Belarus forever. In Europe and the United States he became a very popular artist, producing huge canvasses of dreamlike images in rich colors. In New York City his paintings decorate the lobby of the Metropolitan Opera House. He finally settled in Paris and the themes of his youthful Vitebsk life gradually faded out of his work. He died in 1985.

## MUSIC

Belarus has a long tradition of folk music, which was encouraged during the Soviet era. The Eastern Orthodox Church also has a long tradition of music performed by choirs. Folk music includes special songs for weddings, comic songs, dance tunes, and ballads about past heroes. Several folk choirs perform internationally, and there is an orchestra dedicated to folk music. Typical instruments of Belarusian traditional music are cymbals, pipes, accordions, lyres, and balalaikas, which are triangle-shaped stringed instruments, a little like guitars.

**A group of Belarusian musicians wearing traditional clothes and felt hats.**

*Since 2004, Belarus has been entering performers in the Europe-wide Eurovision Song Contest. A Belarusian singer, Kseniya Sitnik, won the Junior Eurovision Song Contest in 2005.*

Opera and ballet are very popular in Belarus, and the state opera and ballet companies perform regularly. Belarusian composers, including Yuri Semenyako, Yevgeny Glebov, and Heinrich Wagner, have produced operas in musical versions of the socialist realist style. The National Academic Ballet Theater in Minsk is considered one of the foremost ballet companies in the world.

Pop music also flourishes in Belarus with successful Belarusian versions of bands that are popular in Saint Petersburg, Russia. They are unknown outside of Belarus, but thrive in the music scene in the cities. Belarusian pop bands like to play electronic heavy rock, and punk music. Popular bands include Stone People, Dreamlin, and N.R.M. Many rock and music festivals are held all across Belarus and in neighboring Poland, celebrating Belarusian music. In 2002 President Lukashenko passed a law requiring that at least 50 percent of all Belarusian musical radio broadcast music of Belarusian origin.

The elaborate spire of an Orthodox cathedral in Grodno.

## ARCHITECTURE

Ancient buildings are the oldest examples of art in many countries, and even in war-wrecked Belarus, a few ancient buildings have survived. The earliest remaining style of architecture is very simple and can be seen in the 12th-century church of Saints Boris and Gleb in Grodno, with its curved stone apse. A church from the 11th century, the Cathedral of Saint Sophia in Polotsk, also survives. It was damaged by fire in the 15th century, however, and in the 18th century was remodeled in the baroque style. The highly elaborate baroque style was introduced to Belarus under Polish domination in the 17th and 18th centuries.

In the 18th century a classical style of architecture with clean simple lines and minimal decoration was preferred. There was a brief cultural revival in the early 20th century when architects sought to use the traditional folk styles of simple peasant houses, but this impulse quickly gave way to the large—and many feel ugly—buildings of Stalin's era and a rejection of the various indigenous cultures of the Soviet Union. The school of Soviet classicism was a grandiose style with tiers of stonework and ornate columns all designed to create a sense of power and grandeur. The style took earlier ideas and exaggerated them in size and design.

In the late 20th century, housing architecture was plain in design. After World War II, thousands of people needed to be rehoused quickly, and large satellite towns were built with high-rise apartment buildings made with prefabricated parts. To soften the starkness of these buildings, the surroundings were turned into parklands.

## RELIGIOUS ICONS

One of the most ancient forms of art in Belarus is religious iconography. These are miniature paintings, usually on wooden boards, of religious figures such as the Virgin Mary or others from the Bible, or various saints. The Eastern Orthodox Church does not allow three-dimensional figures such as statues, so icons are the main way of decorating church interiors. Icon painting spread from Byzantium (modern-day Turkey) to Eastern Europe and Russia in the 14th century and was used in Belarus both in churches and the home. Simple portraits of religious figures are used as centerpieces on an altar in the home, while in the churches, more elaborate gilded portraits are preferred. In the Middle Ages, most peasants were illiterate, so icons also served as doctrinal storybooks.

In Belarus, icon painting changed over the centuries to include elements from Belarusian folk art and mythology. Often the saints are depicted wearing Belarusian national costume. Common domestic icon illustrations are of Saint Nicholas and of Saint George fighting the dragon.

The screen in front of an altar is called an iconostasis and is covered with magnificently painted icons, or miniature portraits. This iconostasis is from an Orthodox church in Minsk.

## CRAFTS, WOODCARVING, AND CERAMICS

Outside the religious context, art remained primarily a folk tradition until the late 19th century. Woodcarving was a particularly impressive Belarusian skill. In the 15th century, the Russian czar Ivan the Terrible employed Belarusian carpenters and woodcarvers in the construction of his palaces and churches. Other folk art traditions that survive are ceramics and carved wooden toys. The wooden figures are highly elaborate with jointed limbs and delicate painted faces.

Working with straw is also a very old tradition. Boxes and figures are made out of intricately inlaid or woven straw. The most distinctive form of craftwork in Belarus is embroidery on blouses, pinafores, and skirts in traditional styles and on such everyday items as towels and table linens, which are often used for decoration in the home. They are collected by young girls before marriage. Carefully stored, they get displayed on special occasions such as weddings and family parties. Amber is crafted into jewelry and is worn with traditional clothing.

## SOCIALIST REALISM

Marc Chagall abandoned his native land at the same time that socialist realism became the official Soviet art style. In the West, avant-garde art was the dominant art form, with painters expressing emotion rather than making photographic representations of what they saw. On the other hand, in the USSR, Soviet authorities considered art as a form of propaganda, a way of teaching the population about socialism. In 1934 socialist realism was declared the official style for Communist art. The subject matter was to be about the cultivation of the socialist state.

*Above:* **An example of a socialist realist painting in Soviet Russia. Paintings in the socialist realist style were common throughout the Soviet Union for many years. They were forms of propaganda and usually depicted the ideally strong, productive, and dauntless worker or farmer.**

*Opposite:* **A doll made of woven straw in Minsk.**

Initially, the art was optimistic in tone, showing handsome, finely muscled heroes of the revolution building new factories and working on the land, but toward the 1960s it developed a bleaker, less realistic style, taking ideas from the avant-garde and displaying personal images as well as public scenes. Belarus's public places soon filled with such paintings as well as large statues and monuments extolling the grandeur of socialism. As the Soviet Union began to disintegrate, those ponderous statues quickly disappeared all over the USSR and Eastern Europe. In Belarus the paintings were later taken down and replaced with reproductions of impressionists—or even Marc Chagall's lighthearted work.

Many Belarusian artists contributed to the years of socialist realism. One such artist, Mikhail Savitsky, is well known for his painting *Partisan Madonna,* for which he received the silver medal of the Union of Soviet Artists. Other famous painters include Waclaw Sporski, who painted *My Town,* and Sergey Gerasimov, who painted *Belarus: The Partisan's Mother.* Other renowned painters are Zair Azgur, Leonid Shemelev, and Andrei Bembel.

Yakub Kolas is a poet and novelist, and one of the founders of modern Belarusian literature.

## *LITERATURE*

Writing and printing were highly developed in Belarus long before they caught on in the rest of the Slavic world. Francis Skaryna was publishing in the Belarusian language in the early 16th century and was followed 50 years later by Symon Budny, Vasil Cyapinski, and others. In the 17th century, Simeon Polotsky wrote the first poetry in Belarusian. The 19th century saw a cultural renaissance in Belarusian literature. The popular anonymous poem "Taras on Parnassus" is about a peasant who accidentally finds himself in the home of the gods, who are living just like peasants. The poem stands out as a landmark in Belarusian literature because it pointedly implies that the true heart of poetry lies in folk culture, not in the Russian intellectual elite's behavior that dominated Belarusian life at the time.

Under the Russian Empire, however, the use of the Belarusian language was banned and publishing was prohibited. Writing continued but had to be covertly published abroad and under pseudonyms. In 1905 life became a little more liberated under the Russians, and writers again were able to publish in their own language. Two of Belarus's greatest novelists, Yanka Kupala and Yakub Kolas, wrote during this period.

In modern times, literature continues to flourish in Belarus. A union of Belarusian writers was formed in 1932 to support writers, although only writers with politically acceptable works were allowed. Vasil Bykov is now a leading political figure, but he is best known as the writer of novels he published in the 1960s and 1970s. Other renowned modern writers are Vladimir Karatkevich, Anatol Sys, and Ales Razanov. Themes dealing with country life have always dominated Belarusian literature, and that is still true today.

## TWO BELARUSIAN WRITERS

**YANKA KUPALA** (pen name of Ivan Lucevic) was born to a peasant family in 1882 in a small village in central Belarus. He spent his early years moving about with his family in search of work. Early tragedies in his life made him the head of the family at a young age. He had little education and most of his knowledge came from reading books in the private library of a friend.

Lucevic's first efforts at writing were poetry in Polish, but in 1905 he wrote his first works, a series of short stories, in Belarusian. He adopted the pseudonym Yanka Kupala and became a leading member of the group of writers for the magazine *Nasa Niva* (*Our Cornfield*). His body of work includes nature and love poetry, works on social and patriotic themes, four plays, and dramatic and narrative poetry. Although his work declined in the years of Stalin, his peak work is considered the greatest produced in Belarus. Yanka Kupala died in 1942.

**YAKUB KOLAS** Considered the cofounder of modern Belarusian literature, Kanstancin Mickievic also was born in 1882, a child of peasants, in a small village near Minsk. Growing up in the countryside had a profound effect on his work. The family was literate, and Mickievic was educated by his uncle. At first he read in Russian, and his beginning efforts at poetry were in Russian, but later he discovered Belarusian poetry. He attended teacher-training college. His first prose work, using the name Yakub Kolas, was in his local dialect and was about his home village.

As Yakub Kolas read and learned more, he became a revolutionary and was dismissed from college. He wrote a reader for children and went to Vilnius where the magazine *Nasa Niva* published his poetry, which was quite political and satirical at times. He also wrote poetry about nature and peasant life. He wrote novels and allegorical short stories later in his career. He continued producing good works for many years, even in the repressive era of Stalin's rule. Yakub Kolas died in 1956.

# LEISURE

LEISURE PURSUITS IN BELARUS are a mixture of traditional cultural entertainment in rural areas and more sophisticated modern diversions in the cities. Some traditional activities were encouraged during the Soviet era, as were sports. In modern times, all the attractions of the West are beamed in on satellite television. In its quest for tourist dollars, Belarus is also encouraging pastimes such as hiking and wildlife watching in its forests and marshes. New and less restrictive travel rules mean that people now can visit parts of the world they have never before been able to do.

The way people spend their free time in Belarus depends a great deal on their income and work commitments. For some, the new economic circumstances have brought unemployment and increased leisure time—but no money to spend. For others, the challenge of an unfamiliar free-market economy means there are fortunes to be made but little time or opportunity to enjoy their newfound wealth.

*Left:* **A mother and her two children enjoying their walk in a park.**

*Opposite:* **Youths practicing their skateboarding routine in a park.**

## IN THE OUTDOORS

When new cities were on the drawing board in the 1950s and 1960s, the architects were well aware of the disadvantages of city life. Most suburban housing developments therefore are set in green belts with lots of open space and parks for children to play in. Outside the cities, buildings give way to the Belarusian great outdoors of fields, forests, lakes, and rivers. The countryside is beautiful and very distinctive, with vast golden cornfields or huge fields of flax blossoms that are bright blue in summer. With no seacoast, the lakes provide many beaches for sunbathing, picnicking, and swimming and for more luxurious sports such as waterskiing and sailing. One very popular place for residents of Minsk is the Minsk Sea, a dam and reservoir near the city. It is surrounded by woodland walks and picnic areas and is very popular on weekends. Fishing is a widespread activity, too.

**Both lakes and rivers in Belarus are full of succulent fish. These people are trying their luck in the Pripet River.**

## COUNTRY HOUSES

In the old days of the Russian Empire, the upper classes had special homes in the country called dachas, where they would go when Moscow got too hot and sticky or they felt like a rest. Even under the Soviet Union, the dachas remained special retreats for the ruling elite who were the Communist Party officials. Because of its vast forests and good hunting, Belarus has many such dachas located in the countryside. High-ranking Soviet officials would often spend time at them. Several major political treaties of the 1960s and 1970s were in fact signed in Belarusian country houses. Some dachas have over time been turned into sanatoriums or vacation resorts, but there are a great many that are owned by middle-class families who spend their weekends in their cabins and grow much of their own vegetables and fruit.

People enjoy camping in forest reserves. Hunting is a serious sport that incidentally provides a major amount of the meat eaten in Belarus. The forests are so full of wildlife that, unlike other countries that have to protect their forest animals, Belarus can organize hunting tourism. Another favorite activity is gathering food in the forest. Most local people recognize edible mushrooms and berries, and a whole family might spend a day picking the ingredients for delicious jams, jellies, and mushroom stews.

Friends may set up a game of chess in one of the parks if the weather is pleasant.

**Belarusian actresses performing a play in a theater in Gomel.**

## *STORYTELLING AND THEATER*

Leisure pursuits are different for people who live in the country rather than in the cities. What city folk might regard as a hobby, country dwellers usually view as work. In the long historical periods they had little time for leisure pursuits. Evenings would be spent in weaving or preparing food preserves or sewing clothing or mending tools. While involved in these activities, the family and their guests would chat, share news, and tell stories.

Storytelling was an important part of Belarusian life before the arrival of television and is still an essential element of Belarusian culture. Belarusians know many *kaski* (KAH-ski), satirical moral stories that illustrate some aspect of life. There is a story for every occasion. Children have always been taught their lessons about life in this roundabout way. The nature of these stories tells us a lot about the Belarusian character and outlook on life.

There is also a long tradition of traveling theaters in the Belarusian countryside. Ukrainian theater groups were already traveling around in Belarus long before the establishment of The Belarusian Traveling Theater in the 1920s. The most popular entertainments were comic shows or melodramas. Audience participation was a lively part of the shows, with audiences shouting "Look out, he's behind you!" in true vaudevillian fashion as the villain crept up on the hero. A person who attended such a show tells how a character in the play searched in his pockets for a cigarette and a member of the audience actually jumped up and gave him one! Since independence, Belarusian theater has become popular again. Today, there are 27 professional theater groups touring the country as well as 70 orchestras.

## TWO BELARUSIAN STORIES

Belarusians love to tell stories about the supernatural. In many peasant communities people still believe in elves and spirits, and Slavic tales about vampires (corpses that rise at night to drink the blood of the living) have their place in Belarusian mythology. Here are two tales:

**THE WOMAN AND HER CHILD** There once was a woman who grew very tired of constantly carrying her children in her arms. She went to the Great Magician and complained that children cannot walk until they are more than a year old, while lambs, calves, and foals can all walk right after they are born. The Great Magician said that he would help her. He first took a foal and threw it over the hedge. The foal jumped to its feet and ran away. Then he took a lamb and threw it over the hedge. The same thing happened—the lamb got up and gamboled away. Next it was the calf's turn.

Then the magician turned to the woman. "Hand over your child," he ordered. The woman was outraged. "How dare you suggest I throw my child over the fence," she shouted and stormed off in a huff. The magician shrugged, smiled, and went on his way.

**HOW A VAMPIRE CARRIED A GIRL OFF TO THE GRAVE** A young girl and boy very much in love made vows to remain faithful to one another. "If I marry another, let the devil take me," announced the girl.

A year later, another young man came by her house and started to pay her compliments. He was richer and more handsome than her old lover, so the girl broke her engagement and promised to marry her new sweetheart. On the evening before the wedding, a vampire turned up disguised as her former suitor. "Come outside with me, I want to tell you something," he said to the girl. She followed him out and saw a saddled horse. He pulled her up onto the horse and rode away. "There are vampires out tonight. Are you afraid?" he asked. She laughed. "Of course not," she said. A little later he asked again, and she again denied being afraid. Then he told her who he was. They came to some graves and one of them was wide open. The vampire said, "Do you remember your promise? Well, you have broken it, and now I have come for you as you vowed." He unscrewed her head and threw it into the grave, then he followed it down into the earth.

This tale has the moral warning of not breaking promises! The vampire does not suck the girl's blood, as expected, but violently casts away the offending part of her.

*Belarusian stories often feature vampires. However, their vampires, unlike those in Western horror movies, take on different shapes and have pacts with the devil. Not all may suck blood, but they do live in graves and may commit various horrifying deeds such as cutting off a person's head!*

## ENTERTAINMENT IN THE CITIES

There are many things to do in the cities in people's free time. Transportation into the cities is relatively cheap, and in town there are movies and theaters, puppet shows, museums, and cafés that sell alcohol as well as food and are open until late at night. In Minsk alone, the Yanka Kupala Theater, the Russian Drama Theater, the Minsk Puppet Theater, and the State Theater of Musical Comedy are all very popular. Most restaurants have bands or even small orchestras, and a night out with dinner and dancing is a popular evening activity.

For young people, there are discos and music clubs and pizza joints selling foreign beer. Most pop music in Belarus is performed in Russian. An organization called Next Stop-New Life arranges youth festivals, cultural exchanges, and summer camps for young people. There are also many sports stadiums where people can take part in sports or watch games.

# SPORTS

Sports are pursued very earnestly in Belarus. In addition to the many opportunities for watching sporting events, there are 482 sports schools for children and youth, of which 120 are devoted to Olympic sports categories. There are also eight colleges committed to sports. Cross-country skiing is a favorite weekend activity in a land where there is snow cover for over six months of the year.

Young boys playing football (soccer) in Minsk. Their devotion to the sport will remain well into adulthood.

There are several successful basketball players in Belarus, some of whom are currently studying on scholarships in the United States. Vladimir Veremeenko, in particular, has been drafted into the National Basketball Association (NBA) in 2006. In tennis, Vladimir Voltchkov won the 1996 Junior Wimbledon. Two women tennis stars also stand out—Olga Barabanschikova and Natasha Zvereva. The latter has won several titles playing in doubles with Gigi Fernandez from Puerto Rico.

Belarusians have excelled in Olympic sports. Belarus's Olympic committee is headed by President Alexander Lukashenko, a position he has held since 1997. Olga Korbut and Nelli Kim, both world-renowned names in gymnastics, are from Belarus, while the two strongest men in the world, Alexander Kurlovich and Leonid Taranenko, are also Belarusian. In the Atlanta Olympics in 1996, Belarus competed for the second time as a nation and did very well. Many of the athletes competed wearing the red and white colors of their newly independent state, while others wore the colors of the old Soviet flag, red and yellow. The great athlete Vitaly Scherbo—the first person in Olympic history to win four gold medals in one day, the winner of six Olympic gold medals at the 1992

Barcelona Olympics, for a total of 14 World gold medals—also won four bronze medals for all-around gymnastics, the horizontal bar, the parallel bars, and the vault at Atlanta. Other Belarusian athletes also won medals. Scherbo now lives in the United States. In the 2000 Summer Olympics in Sydney, the country won 17 medals, including three gold medals. More recently, in the 2004 Summer Olympics in Athens, Belarus took home 15 medals, including two gold medals. One of those was claimed by Yulia Nestsiarenka, who is the current Women's Olympic 100-meter champion.

Ice hockey is without doubt the nation's most popular sport. Several thousand youths study it at special sports schools, and there is a Golden Puck tournament for boys from ages 10 to 14. The Belarusian national team finished fourth in the 2002 Olympics in Salt Lake City. Arguably their greatest moment came in that competition, when they beat Sweden in the quarter finals in a very close game. Many Belarusian athletes play for National Hockey League (NHL) teams in the United States, and in Canada. In 2007 the national team was ranked ninth in the world.

## THE MEDIA

In Belarus, almost everyone owns a TV set, and some may own two or three. Belarusian people watch their state-owned national TV channel —Belarusian National State Teleradio Company—as well as Russian TV channels. Of these, one is an independent channel. The Russian independent channel received in Belarus, NTV, includes in its programming investigative news shows as well as political debates, but for the most part news is presented by state television. Belarusian television broadcasts in a mixture of the Belarusian and Russian languages. In the southern and western parts of the country viewers can pick up Polish and Ukrainian stations, too. A few viewers have access to satellite television or cable, but most of those programs are in foreign languages. The chief barrier to ownership of a satellite is the high cost of the equipment rather than lack of interest in the service.

Watching television has become a major daily activity just as it has in the West. Several Western soap operas and situation comedies have found their way onto Belarusian TV screens. Satellite television is uncensored, unlike state channels. Programs tend to include lots of variety and cultural shows, movies, some foreign TV series, and news broadcasts. Russian and Belarusian soaps deal with themes similar to Western ones—love triangles, family relationships, and sometimes more challenging moral issues. Old Western movies are dubbed or subtitled. Many young Belarusians are as interested in the lives of movie stars such as Tom Cruise or Matt Damon as are their counterparts in the United States.

Radio is also popular. There are three government-run national radio stations, and many foreign radio stations can be received, especially from neighboring Poland and Lithuania.

Some 460 newspapers and magazines are published regularly in Belarus, of which 150 or so are in Belarusian and a similar number are in Russian. The rest are issued in a mixture of the two principal languages or in the minority languages—Polish, Ukrainian, or English. State subsidies are given to magazines or newspapers that are published in Belarusian and to those involved in the arts or that are produced for children. The most popular daily newspapers are *Sovetskaya Belorossiya* (the main Russian language daily), *Narodnaya Volya* (the main opposition daily), and the bilingual *Narodnaya Hazeta*, published in Russian and Belarusian. *Belorusskaya Niva* is in Russian.

*The Lukashenko regime keeps a close eye on press reportage in Belarus, and newspapers that have been critical of the government—such as the* Belaruskaya Delovaya Gazeta—*have been targeted for closure.*

# FESTIVALS

FOR THE 70 OR SO YEARS that Belarus was a part of the USSR, most of its traditional festivals were very quietly observed, if at all. In the early years of the Russian Revolution, priests were tried and imprisoned, and Christian and other festivals publicly mocked. People were expected to attend the Soviet parades and celebrations for the October Revolution. But religions were never completely outlawed, and the few spared churches and synagogues throughout the Soviet Union continued to observe their major festivals. Christian churches still rang church bells, while many people stood quietly nearby to listen to them.

In today's Belarus, many people of all religions are rediscovering their cultural roots and traditional festivals are appearing once again. Modern celebrations in Belarus include music and arts festivals.

*Belarusians celebrate their independence on July 3, the day in 1944 the country was liberated from the Nazi army occupation by the Soviet Red Army during World War II.*

*Left:* **A group of graceful women performing a traditional dance in a park.**

*Opposite:* **A woman costumed as a flower during a local festival.**

Townspeople join hands and dance in a large circle around the bonfire during the Kupalle festival.

*Yanka Kupala, a famous writer and poet in the 19th century, derived his pen name from Kupalle, since he was born at the time of summer solstice.*

## TRADITIONAL FESTIVALS

Many festivals that date back to pre-Christian times are still celebrated in Belarus. Winter and summer solstices are very important.

**KUPALLE** The festival of Kupalle (koo-PAH-leh) is held around the summer solstice in June and celebrates nature and the joys of summertime. It is thought to be named after a pagan goddess. People return to their home villages to participate in the fields and forests with picnics and bonfires. Traditional songs are sung and performed on ancient Belarusian instruments. People dance in *karagods* (KAH-rah-gods), that is, in circles around the bonfires. A popular pastime during the festivities is to search for a particular fern that rarely flowers—if found, it is believed to bring good luck. There is a saying that if one falls in love during Kupalle, the marriage will be a very happy one.

**KALIADY** The winter solstice, Kaliady (kal-ee-AD-ee), is celebrated just before Christmas and is more popular even than Kupalle. Groups of young people dress up in traditional clothes and wear masks depicting animals, in particular, sheep. They carry a board with a sun on it, perhaps to remind everyone that the worst of the long, cold winter is over and the sun will soon rise up strong again. Boisterous parties of young revelers visit house to house, singing and dancing, and displaying the sheep's mask to the head of each household. Each home offers them food and drink in return.

**HARVEST FESTIVAL** Another ancient festival is the harvest festival, Dozinkyoi (dozsh-INK-yah), when farmers proclaim the successful completion of the harvest. People will travel home to their villages to join in the much-loved festivities. A huge party is held where everyone enjoys food from the summer harvest, and the tables are decorated with buckets of flowers and herbs. Traditional songs are sung, and village folk dance around bonfires.

**TIDYING OF GRAVES** Another ancient tradition in Belarus that predates Christianity is the annual tidying of graves. It is performed at different times of the year by different groups. Catholics observe this on November 2, Remembrance Day or All Souls' Day, called Dzyady (TSYAH-dee). Orthodox Christians celebrate the festival at the Easter of the Dead, held the Thursday after Orthodox Easter, called Radovniza (RAH-doh-nit-sah). At these times relatives travel to the graves of their parents and grandparents to tidy the tombs, light candles, and to leave some food and drinks. Some families take a share of their painted Easter eggs to the grave to confirm that the ancestor is still a part of the family. At the grandfather's grave some vodka is often left.

Exuberant dancing celebrates Kaliady, the winter festival.

*Christmas is calculated by a different calendar in the Orthodox Church and is observed on January 7 instead of on December 25.*

## CHRISTIAN FESTIVALS

The Orthodox and Roman Catholic Churches follow different calendars and thus celebrate the religious holidays on different dates. Easter is the most important religious occasion in the Orthodox Church. It falls at least 13 days after the Catholic Easter. It must also always follow the Jewish Passover festival. Easter is preceded by the long period of Lent, which is a time of fasting and penitence in Eastern Orthodoxy and Catholicism alike.

The rituals for Easter begin the week before Easter Sunday with a service of forgiveness. On Good Friday there is a procession of the Epitahion (ep-it-AH-hyon) or the laying out of the body of Christ. The next service is the blessing of fire and a service of vigil. Easter begins

## NATIONAL AND RELIGIOUS HOLIDAYS

| | |
|---|---|
| January 1 | New Year |
| January 7 | Orthodox Christmas |
| March 8 | International Women's Day |
| March 15 | Constitution Day |
| March/April | Roman Catholic Easter |
| March/April | Eastern Orthodox Easter |
| April 23 (variable) | Easter of the Dead |
| May 1 | Labor Day |
| May 9 | Victory Day (commemorating the end of World War II) |
| June 21 | Kupalle (summer solstice) |
| July 3 | Independence Day |
| November 2 | Remembrance Day (war dead and ancestor memorial) |
| December 21 | Kaliady (winter solstice) |
| December 25 | Roman Catholic Christmas |

## EASTER EGGS

While Easter is celebrated as a Christian festival, many ancient traditions are associated with it. Eggs symbolize new life, and painted eggs are a very old Easter tradition, especially in Eastern Europe, reaching back to a time when rustic people rejoiced at the birth of a new growing season. In the ancient religions, this time of year would have been very significant.

In Belarus, Easter is a time for a whole family to assemble at their parents' house for a big meal. A special round cake is baked, and a single hen's egg is elaborately decorated in red. People take the egg and the cake to church for the Eucharistic celebration, where they are blessed. Then, after the family meal, the egg and cake are cut up to give each member of the family an equal share to symbolize the unity of the family.

with a procession that symbolizes the search for the body of Christ. When the procession starts, the church is left in darkness, but when it returns and the resurrection is announced, thousands of candles and other lights are lit. The sacrament of Eucharist (communion) is given early on Easter Sunday morning. Eastern Orthodox processions and services are highly ornate and complex events with the priests wearing elaborate vestments, and treasured icons and other holy paintings being reverently carried.

Easter is a very important occasion for Catholics as well. On Easter Sunday there are many colorful processions, and the faithful light candles to commemorate the resurrection of Jesus Christ.

A local priest holding a venerable Bible during a Christian festival in Belarus.

The Orthodox Christmas is held in January, while the Catholic Christmas is celebrated in December, which is also the time for the traditional pre-Christian festival of Kaliady. Some Kaliady customs have been assimilated into Christmas observances.

## JEWISH FESTIVALS

The Jewish community today in Belarus is very small. During the Soviet era many Jewish people soft-pedaled their religion in order to avoid persecution. Today there is a revival of Judaism, and many young people are seeking out the religious festivals of their culture. The spring feast of the Passover commemorates the ancient exodus of the Israelite tribe from Egypt. The festival, which lasts for eight days, begins with a devout family gathering for the Passover seder. Prayers and songs are followed by a meal with many symbolic dishes. Bitter herbs are passed around and tasted to remind the family of the pain of bondage. Roast lamb is eaten to recall the offerings of the Israelites, and matzo bread commemorates the unleavened bread eaten by them on their exodus from Egypt, where they had been heavily persecuted.

The next festival in the Jewish year is Shavuot, which acknowledges the giving of the Ten Commandments to Moses. The Feast of the Tabernacles, Yom Kippur, or the Day of Atonement, and the Feast of Lots are also observed during the year.

## SOVIET CELEBRATIONS

As part of the USSR, Belarus took part in many official Soviet holidays, along with the other republics. Many of these festivals are still celebrated by Belarus and its neighbors to the east and west. May Day and the October Revolution were two big national events in the Soviet Union, highlighted with massive displays of weapons and the heavy products of industry. May Day, now called Labor Day in Belarus, is a traditional day for rejoicing in both the arrival of spring and the hard-won rights of working people. A much more popular public event is the festival on July 27 to remember the brief period of independence in 1917.

*Under Soviet domination, attendance at May Day parades was compulsory. Nowadays, May 1 often comes and goes quietly, with some people watching the Labor Day parade or just staying at home or going to visit their parents or friends.*

## MUSIC FESTIVALS

Belarus also took part in other holidays under the USSR, including various music festivals. During these, traditional music, opera, and classical music performers from all over the USSR would be gathered together in one of the Soviet capitals. The USSR also conducted celebrations of Soviet art, literature, poetry, dance, and many other aspects of their culture. Performances of music and displays of art from the other Soviet republics were taken to Belarus as part of these festivals, and friendly competitions would take place.

In 1972 a poetry day was started, on which poets throughout Belarus would read their works. In 1974 a Minsk Festival of Music was organized, and the popular festival continues to this day. Held in the last 10 days of November every year, the entertainments feature Belarusian music, including diverse performances from drum majorettes to jazz to rock to time-honored music and dancing. Many musicians perform in their traditional folk costumes. The Lukashenko government has continued the Soviet practice of sponsoring these national festivals.

Dressed as brides, dancers perform at the Minsk Festival of Music.

# FOOD

BELARUSIAN FOOD is totally unknown in the West. It is a home-style cuisine that uses local ingredients. Traditionally, a large clay stove was used for cooking. Although this type of stove is no longer in use, the style of dishes—slowly baked or stewed—remains popular. As in other peasant fare, bulk is what is important rather than delicacy of taste. Belarusian dishes are based on the staples—bread, potatoes, cabbage, and pork, with mushrooms as an important ingredient in stuffing and sauces. Meat patties and *pirozhki* (pierogi, small pies stuffed with meat, cheese, or vegetables) and fruit pies are also frequently served.

*Above:* **There are now private markets selling fruits and vegetables, such as this one in Grodno.**

*Opposite:* **Local fruits and pastries tempt passersby at a fair in Belarus.**

In Soviet times, the price of food was highly regulated and was only a small part of the family's budget. Public canteens in every town served workers cheap, wholesome food for lunch. The main family meal was in the evening. In modern times this situation has changed a great deal, and people have experienced price increases and occasional food shortages. Small plots of land and gardens at home have become very important, and in unofficial markets vegetables and other foods change hands. The accident at Chernobyl has, of course, added enormously to the problems, since large areas of cultivated land had to be abandoned. Livestock, wild animals that were once hunted for food, and the plant produce of the southern forests were all contaminated, and now people have to guard against the danger of such food getting into the marketplace.

Fasting is an important part of the Eastern Orthodox religious cycle. At times of the year such as the 40 days and nights of Lent, people have to give up meat and dairy products. Just before Lent, therefore, all the fresh meat and dairy in the house are used up, and the faithful start eating mostly vegetable dishes.

Presenting bread and salt is a traditional form of hospitality for Belarusians, particularly when visiting a new home.

## *BREAD*

One of the main food staples in Belarus is bread. White bread is popular in the cities and in the southern part of the country. One type of this bread is known as *kalachi* (kal-AH-chi), a small loaf baked in the shape of a padlock. But the commonest form of bread is wholemeal rye bread. In the old days, the dough would have been baked in the embers of the oven, then placed on cabbage or maple leaves, covered with a cloth to cool, and sprinkled with salt before eating.

Belarus has to import much of its wheat, partly due to the effects of Chernobyl and partly because the short wet summers make growing wheat difficult. Since rye is a much easier crop and is widely grown in Belarus, rye bread is much more universally eaten.

There have been many traditions associated with bread and its production in Belarus. Small pieces of the dough were given to children so that they could make their own small roll. Another traditional usage was to call any bread brought home uneaten from the day's farm work "hare's bread," meaning of little importance, after the nickname of the ruble (which features a hare on the note), the second-smallest unit of money. If one dropped a piece of bread, it was customary to pick it up saying, "Lord forgive me!"

## *POTATOES*

Potatoes are the main staple of the Belarusian diet and are grown in much of the country. There are a great many different ways of cooking potatoes in Belarus. The simplest method is to put them in the ashes of a fire until the potatoes are baked. After cooking, the flesh is scooped out, sprinkled with salt, and eaten with butter or flax oil.

There are also more elaborate ways of cooking potatoes. One method is to make dumplings from grated potatoes that are then stuffed with meat or mushrooms and baked in the oven. The dumplings are usually served as a side dish to meat.

Another common way of preparing grated potatoes is to shape them into pancakes called *dranniki* (DRAN-ih-ki), fry them with mushrooms, and serve them with sour cream and often a side dish of pickled berries. Potato pies are also popular.

## MEAT DISHES

Pork is the most popular meat in traditional Belarusian cooking. Pig farming is carried out largely on factory farms, where pork is processed

**Men ice fishing on a frozen lake in Belarus, a seasonal recreation that also yields abundant fresh food.**

into bacon, ham, and sausages. A much-loved pork dish is *kotleta pokrestyansky* (kot-LET-ah polk-ress-tee-AN-skee)—pork cutlets served in mushroom sauce. Another well-liked dish in modern times and authentically Belarusian is *machanka* (mah-CHAN-kah), which is a thickened spicy gravy, with pieces of pork, served with pancakes. Beefsteak, although a luxurious meal, is widely enjoyed, too. The markets also offer wild game such as duck, pheasant, and geese; these are roasted or baked in earthenware pots and served with wild berry sauce. Lake and river fish, including perch, bream, loach, and crayfish (a crustacean) are plentiful and are served at home and in restaurants. Fish roe is a popular delicacy but can be very expensive.

Russian cuisine is also quite common in a country where a large proportion of the population is ethnic Russian.

Sausages are a popular Belarusian food.

## KITCHENS

People in Belarus today have many modern appliances in their kitchens. Up-to-date gas or electric stoves are used for most cooking, and refrigerators keep food fresh. All sorts of canned and frozen foods can be bought at supermarkets. Many people eat out, especially townspeople at lunchtime.

In the countryside, many modern houses are still built with a big cellar or an icehouse in the yard. Icehouses have been used since the 15th century in Belarus for cold storage of vegetables and preserves. Known as *ledniks* (LED-niks), they are built of bricks and are covered with earth. Often grass grows over the tops of them. Ice blocks cut from rivers and lakes and placed in them during winter may stay frozen well into the summer months.

## SWEETS AND DRINKS

Typical traditional sweet dishes in Belarus are pies made from such local fruits as apples or berries. Grapes are grown in the south as well as pears and strawberries. In modern Belarus, ice cream is a favorite treat, and Pinguin is a very successful chain of ice-cream parlors. Gingerbread and cakes made with honey are also typical desserts.

The traditional drink of Belarus is birch juice. But more common nowadays is a slightly alcoholic drink called kvass—not to be confused with the soup of the same name. It is made from malt, flour, sugar, mint,

## A PEASANT'S DELIGHT

They brought on sauerkraut at first
Then soup with scratchings, piping hot.
Stiff millet-porridge then was served—
Make free with it and eat the lot!
Then jelly and yogurt, nice and cool,
And gruel with pork fat swimming round,
And roasted geese, in a buttery pool,
Enough for all the gods was found.
And then they served fine sausages too,
And oatmeal pancakes by the score.
Taras wept tears of joy anew.

This is part of a 19th-century poem, "Taras on Parnassus," and describes some courses of a fine traditional meal. First is an appetizer, in this case, sauerkraut, a pickled cabbage often served cold in a kind of soup called *kapusta* (kah-POOS-tah).

The next course would be a hot soup. There are many kinds to choose from. *Poliuka* (POLL-yoo-kah) is a hot soup thickened with flour. *Prantsak* (pran-SAHK) is made from pearl barley and mushrooms. Other popular soups are made from potatoes seasoned with pork rinds, or a combination of noodles and chicken giblets. In spring, sorrel soup is a favorite, as is nettle soup made from the common wayside plant. *Kvass* (KVAHS) falls somewhere between a soup and a drink. As a soup, it is made from beets, with meat, mushrooms, and vegetables added. A more common soup in modern Belarus is borscht, a plain beet soup that originated in the Ukraine and is served with dollops of sour cream.

Jelly and yogurt would be side dishes to enhance the taste of the food and to clear the palate from one course to the next. The main course at this meal is goose, a quite rare dish at a peasant's table, since waterfowl were valuable stock and not often slaughtered.

and fruit. *Belovezhskaya* (bel-ov-VYEH-skah-yah) is one of many widely used herbal drinks believed to have a medicinal value. Apple cider, drinks made from honey, and locally brewed beer are also drunk, along with local versions of trendy fizzy drinks. Tea is usually drunk without milk. It is still a common drink, but coffee is becoming more popular. Alcohol is served in cafés and restaurants as well as in bars, but the law restricts the quantity of vodka that can be served with food. Belarusians have bigger incomes in recent years, and bottled water and sports-type energy drinks are now more in demand in the towns and cities.

## PIERNIK

½ pound (225 g) ground nuts
½ cup (160 g) jam
1 cup (200 g) sugar
1 large egg
½ teaspoon (2 ml) pure vanilla extract
½ teaspoon (2 ml) baking soda
3 cups (375 g) all-purpose flour

Preheat the oven to 350°F (180°C). Mix in a large bowl the nuts, jam, sugar, egg, vanilla, and baking soda until the mixture is a smooth paste. Add the flour, then mix and knead into a dough. Roll out the dough and shape it into a round cake. Place it on a greased and floured baking sheet and bake for 45 minutes, or until browned. Serves 6.

## COUNTRY BEEF STEW

1 pound (approximately 450 g) of stewing beef, cut into one-inch cubes
2 tablespoons (15 g) flour
salt
pepper
3 tablespoons (45 ml) cooking oil
1 cup (250 ml) beef stock
6 medium potatoes, peeled and cut into ¼-inch slices
2 carrots, coarsely chopped
2 sticks celery, sliced diagonally
4 small onions, chopped finely
3.5 fluid ounces (approximately 100 ml) sour cream
3 bay leaves

Place the flour in a shallow bowl and season with salt and pepper to taste. Lightly roll the cubed beef in the flour until evenly coated. Now brown the meat in the oil over medium-high heat until crisp. Transfer the meat to a pot. Pour a little stock into the pan and scrape up any brown bits. Add to the pot and cover the meat with stock. Bring to a boil, then cover and simmer for 90 minutes. Replenish the stock at intervals to make sure the liquid does not steam away.

Add the bay leaves, celery, carrots, potatoes, and onions to the pot and cook for 20 minutes more. Add the sour cream and simmer for another five minutes. Serve hot. Serves 6.

**LATVIA**

Lake Osveyskoye

*Polotsk Lowland*

Western Dvina

● Polotsk

● Vitebsk

**RUSSIA**

**LITHUANIA**

*Lake Naroch*

● Orsha

*Dnieper*

● Vilnius

*Oshmyany Upland*

*B e l a r u s i a n   R i d g e*

● Mogilev

MINSK ●

▲ Dzerzhinska Mountain
(1,135 ft / 346 m)

● Bykhov

*Svisloch*

*Neman*

*Belovezhskaya Forest Nature Reserve*

● Grodno

*Neman Lowland*

● Bobruisk

● Slutsk

*Central Berezina Plain*

*Berezina*

*Dnieper*

● Soligorsk

*Berezina Nature Reserve*

Gomel ●

**POLAND**

*Lowland*

*Pripet Nature Reserve*

*Pripet*

*Bug*

*Pripet Marshes*

● Pinsk

● Brest

*Dnieper*

Chernobyl ●

**U K R A I N E**

| | Capital city |
| --- | --- |
| ● | Major town |
| ▲ | Mountain peak |

| Feet | | Meters |
| --- | --- | --- |
| 16,500 | | 5,000 |
| 9,900 | | 3,000 |
| 6,600 | | 2,000 |
| 3,300 | | 1,000 |
| 1,650 | | 500 |
| 660 | | 200 |
| 0 | | 0 |

# MAP OF BELARUS

Belarusian Ridge, A3, B2–B3, C2
Belovezhskaya Forest Nature Reserve, A3
Berezina Nature Reserve, C3, D3
Berezina River, C3, D3
Bobruisk, C3
Brest, A4
Bug River, A4
Bykhov, C3

Central Berezina Plain, C3
Chernobyl (Ukraine), D4

Dnieper Lowland, C3–C4, D3–D4
Dnieper River, C2, D2–D4
Dzerzhinska Mountain, B3

Gomel, D3
Grodno, A3

Lake Naroch, B2
Lake Osveyskoye, B1
Latvia, A1, B1
Lithuania, A1–A3, B1–B2

Minsk, B3
Mogilev, D2

Neman Lowland, A3
Neman River, A3, B3

Orsha, C2
Oshmyany Upland, B2

Pinsk, B4
Poland, A2–A5
Polotsk, C1
Polotsk Lowland, B1
Pripet Marshes, B4
Pripet Nature Reserve, C4
Pripet River, B4, C4

Russia, B1, C1, D1–D4

Slutsk, B3
Soligorsk, B3
Svisloch River, B2–B3, C3

Ukraine, A4–A5, B4–B5, C4–C5, D4–D5

Vilnius (Lithuania), A2
Vitebsk, C1

Western Dvina River, B1–C1

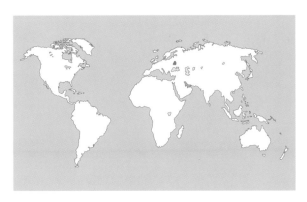

# ECONOMIC BELARUS

## Manufacturing

- Gas processing
- Machine tools
- Metallurgy
- Synthetic polymer fiber plant
- Oil refining
- Textiles
- Vehicles
- Wood processing

## Agriculture

- Dairy farming
- Flax
- Oats
- Pig farming
- Potatoes
- Sugar beets
- Wheat

## Natural Resources

- Coal
- Oil fields
- Peat
- Phosphorite
- Potash

## Services

- Airport
- Scientific research

# ABOUT THE ECONOMY

## OVERVIEW

The economy of Belarus is highly industrialized and dependent on imported energy and raw materials, especially from neighboring Russia. Despite nearly 20 years of independence from the Soviet Union, the country's economy is still tightly controlled by the government and runs along old-style socialist lines. Farms are still run as collectives, most factories are state-supervised, and prices are set by the government. A large part of the national budget is spent on social programs. Private businesses are highly regulated, which has discouraged foreign investment. Even with these impediments, the economy has been growing steadily in recent years, and trade with Europe has increased. Belarus receives heavily discounted oil and natural gas from Russia, and much of Belarus's growth can be attributed to the reexport of Russian oil after refining, at more expensive world market prices. This arrangement of discounts is likely to be retired in years to come, however, causing energy prices in Belarus to increase rapidly and the economy to become slower.

## GROSS DOMESTIC PRODUCT (GDP)
US $31.7 billion (2007 estimate)

## GROWTH RATE
6.9 percent (2007 estimate)

## INFLATION RATE
8.3 percent (2007 estimate)

## CURRENCY
Belarusian ruble (2,145 rubles = US $1 in 2007)

## UNEMPLOYMENT RATE
1.6 percent officially registered

## MAIN EXPORTS
Machinery and equipment, mineral products, chemicals, petrochemicals, metals, textile, and foodstuffs

## MAIN EXPORT PARTNERS
Russia 34.7 percent, Netherlands 17.7 percent, United Kingdom 7.5 percent, Ukraine 6.3 percent, Poland 5.2 percent

## MAIN IMPORTS
Energy (oil and gas), raw materials, manufactured goods, wheat

## MAIN IMPORT PARTNERS
Russia 58.6 percent, Germany 7.5 percent, Ukraine 5.5 percent

## AGRICULTURAL PRODUCTS
Wheat, potatoes, sugar beets, flax, beef, milk, vegetables

## INDUSTRIAL PRODUCTS
Metal-cutting machine tools, tractors, trucks, earthmovers, motorcycles, television sets, chemical fibers, fertilizer, textiles, radios, refrigerators

## CELL PHONES
5.96 million (2006)

## INTERNET USERS
5.5 million (2006)

## AIRPORTS
67 (2007 estimate), including 36 paved

# CULTURAL BELARUS

**Minsk Stalinist architecture**
Much of modern-day Minsk was built in the Stalinist-era architectural style dating from the 1930s to the1950s. Highlights include the prewar Independence Square, which features a statue of Lenin and the Belarusian State University building; the GUM department store; October Square; and the Trade Unions' Palace of Culture.

**Victory Square**
In the center of downtown Minsk, the massive Victory Square honors the Soviet victory in World War II. At the center of the square is a star-topped monument with an eternal flame to commemorate the war dead.

**Belovzheskaya Pushcha National Park**
Belarus's largest national park is home to many rare European animals, such as the European bison, or wisent, as well as some of the oldest primeval forests in Europe.

**Brest Fortress**
This large fortress is a monument to one of the great, if little known, sieges of World War II when, in June and July 1941, a regiment of brave Soviet soldiers without hope of relief kept German forces at bay until their supplies finally ran out.

**Great Patriotic War Museum**
A place of somber remembrance in the heart of Minsk, this museum records the most tragic period in Belarus's modern history, the brutal three-year Nazi occupation. Many atrocities are recorded in photographs and dioramas.

**Minsk churches**
Although much of Minsk was destroyed in World War II, some famous churches, with impressive architecture and incomparable icons, survived, including the Roman Catholic Church of Saints Simon and Elena. Also standing is one of the most recognizable symbols of Minsk, the 17th-century Orthodox Holy Spirit Cathedral.

**Dudutki**
This open-air museum is dedicated to the culture and natural resources of Belarus. It includes workshops demonstrating the vanished ways of life, ancient technologies, and traditional arts and crafts.

**National Academy of Sciences**
This outdoor site contains a unique collection of more than 2000 glacial boulders and rocks, dating from many thousands of years ago.

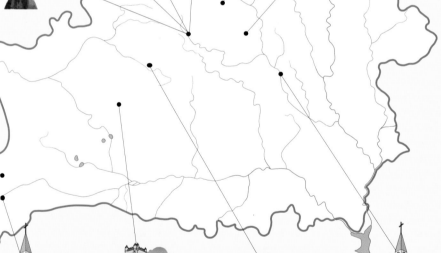

**Holy Resurrection Church**
The largest place of worship in Belarus, this handsome five-domed Orthodox church can accommodate up to 5,000 people.

**Niasvizh Castle**
This 16th-century castle was developed into a chateau by Mikolaj Krysztof Radziwill in the 16th century. The architecture is an impressive mixture of Renaissance and Baroque styles. The castle is a national cultural reserve and a UNESCO World Heritage site.

**Mirsky Castle complex**
Dating from the 15th century, the castle complex near the town of Mir has impressive Renaissance architectural features. Much of the castle was restored in the 19th century, when new details were added.

**Borisov**
Borisov is home to a beautiful 19th-century orthodox church and a monument commemorating the final battle in November 1812 between Russian and French forces in the Napoleonic invasion of Russia.

# ABOUT THE CULTURE

**OFFICIAL NAME**
Respublika Byelarus (Republic of Belarus)

**NATIONAL FLAG**
A red horizontal band at the top and a green horizontal band half the width of the red band; a white vertical stripe on the hoist side has a Belarusian traditional decorative pattern in red.

**NATIONALITY**
Belarusian

**CAPITAL**
Minsk

**LAND AREA**
80,155 square miles (207,600 square km)

**POPULATION**
9,685,768 (2008 estimate)

**ADMINISTRATIVE DISTRICTS (VOBLASTS)**
Minsk, Pinsk, Grodno, Gomel, Vitebsk, Mogilev, Brest

**HIGHEST POINT**
Dzyarzhynskaya Mountain (1,135 feet/346 m)

**MAJOR RIVERS**
Dnieper, Western Dvina, Neman, Western Bug, Pripyat, Sozh, Berezina, Vilija, Ptsich, Shchara, Svislach

**MAJOR LAKES**
More than 11,000 lakes, the largest of which are Lake Naroch and Lake Osveyskoye

**PRINCIPAL LANGUAGES**
Belarusian, Russian

**ETHNIC GROUPS**
Belarusian 81.2 percent, Russian 11.4 percent, Polish 3.9 percent, Ukrainian 2.4 percent, others 1.1 percent (1999 census)

**MAJOR RELIGIONS**
Eastern Orthodox 80 percent, others 20 percent, including Roman Catholic, Protestant, Jewish, and Muslim

**FERTILITY RATE**
1.23 children born per woman (2008 estimate)

**BIRTHRATE**
9.62 births per thousand (2008 estimate)

**INFANT MORTALITY RATE**
6.53 deaths per thousand live births (2008 estimate)

**LIFE EXPECTANCY**
64.63 years, male; 76.4 years female (2008 estimate)

**LITERACY RATE**
99.6 percent of population age 15 and over

# TIME LINE

| IN BELARUS | IN THE WORLD |
|---|---|

**323 B.C.**
Alexander the Great's empire stretches from Greece to India.

**A.D. 200s**
Slavs inhabit the region and trade with the Roman Empire.

**1067**
Earliest records of Minsk date to this period. Prince Useslau rules over principality of Polotsk.

**1200s**
Belarus enfolded by Lithuania.

**1206–1368**
Genghis Khan unifies the Mongols and starts conquest of the world. At its height, the Mongol Empire under Kublai Khan stretches from China to Persia and parts of Europe and Russia.

**1392**
Vytautas takes over the Belarusian throne.

**1697**
The Union of Lublin bans the Belarusian language in official contexts.

**1789–99**
The French Revolution

**1793**
Russia completes its takeover of Belarus.

**1919**
The Byelorussian Soviet Socialist Republic is proclaimed.

**1914**
World War I begins.

**1921**
The Treaty of Riga divides Belarus between Poland and Soviet Russia.

**1922**
The Belarusian Soviet Socialist Republic becomes a founding member of the Union of Soviet Socialist Republics (USSR).

**1941**
Nazi Germany invades Belarus during World War II. More than 1 million people are killed during the occupation, including many Jews.

**1939**
World War II begins.

**1944**
The Soviet Red Army drives the Germans out of Belarus.

**1945**
At the end of the war, much of western Belarus—previously belonging to Poland—is amalgamated into the Belorussian Soviet Socialist Republic.

**1945**
The United States drops atomic bombs on Hiroshima and Nagasaki.

**1986**
Belarus is heavily affected by radioactive fallout from the massive nuclear explosion at Chernobyl in neighboring Ukraine. A quarter of the nation's agricultural land is contaminated.

**1986**
Nuclear power disaster at Chernobyl in Ukraine

| IN BELARUS | IN THE WORLD |
|:---:|:---:|

**1988**

Belarusian Popular Front is formed as part of the nationalist revival prompted by Soviet leader Mikhail Gorbachev's policy of "openness."

**1991**

Belarus declares its independence as the Soviet Union breaks up.

**1994**

Alexander Lukashenko becomes president of Belarus.

**1995**

A friendship and cooperation pact is signed with Russia. National referenda result in the restoration of Russian as an official language. The president's powers are also widened.

**1996**

An agreement on economic union is signed with Russia. Lukashenko further increases his powers, extending his term of office.

**1997**

Hong Kong is returned to China.

**2001**

Alexander Lukashenko is reelected to serve a second term.

**2003**

War in Iraq begins.

**2004**

Referendum backs change, allowing the president to serve more than the previous limit of two terms. Opposition parties fail to win a single seat in parliamentary elections.

**2005**

Diplomatic row with Poland over treatment of ethnic Poles accused of stirring up unrest in a bid to overthrow President Lukashenko.

**2006**

President Lukashenko is declared the winner by a landslide in elections condemned as rigged by Western observers. Dozens arrested at opposition demonstrations in Minsk.

**2007**

Russia cuts oil supply through an oil export pipeline to Europe amid a row with Belarus over taxation and allegations of siphoning. The dispute ends after Russia agrees to reduce the oil duty it charges Belarus.

# GLOSSARY

**andraki** (and-RARK-ee)
Woolen winter skirts.

**banya** (BAN-yah)
Rustic bathhouse similar to a sauna.

**dacha**
Country house.

**glasnost**
Openness.

**ice age**
Any period of time during which glaciers covered a large part of the earth's surface.

**icon**
Miniature religious image typically painted on a wooden panel depicting a scene from the Bible or a religious figure.

**kalachi** (kal-AH-chi)
Small loaf of bread baked in the shape of a padlock.

**karagods** (KAH-rah-gods)
Circles formed around bonfires by festive dancers.

**kaski** (KAH-ski)
An entertaining fable with a moral.

**Krivichi**
Slavic tribe that lived in the Belarus region in the early centuries A.D.

**Kupalle**
Summer solstice festival in Belarus with pagan origins.

**kvass**
Mildly alcoholic drink made from fermented malt, flour, mint, and fruit.

**lednik** (LED-nik)
Icehouse to store vegetables and preserves.

**perestroika**
More liberal economic changes in the USSR in the 1980s under Mikhail Gorbachev.

**Polonization**
The process of converting a country's language and culture to a Polish one.

**rayon** (ray-ON)
A district of Belarus (there are 141 *rayoni*).

**Russification**
The process of changing a country's language and culture to Russian culture.

**Soviet**
A name used to describe the style of government or cultural aspects of the Soviet Union. It is also the name of the elected council in Belarus (although its continued existence is questionable).

**Tatars**
A group of Muslim people who first came to Eastern Europe from Central Asia in the 11th century.

**trasyanka** (traz-YAN-kah)
A language of mixed Russian and Belarusian grammar and vocabulary, spoken throughout Belarus.

**UNESCO**
United Nations Educational, Scientific, and Cultural Organization.

**voblasti** (VOH-blahst-EE)
Regional divisions.

# FURTHER INFORMATION

**BOOKS**

Richmond, Simon et al. *Russia and Belarus (Lonely Planet Country Guide)*. Oakland, CA: Lonely Planet Publications, 2006.

Roberts, Nigel. *Belarus (Country Guides)*. Chalfont St. Peter, UK: Bradt Publications, 2006.

Walker, Linda. *Living After Chernobyl: Ira's Story (Children in Crisis)*. New York: World Almanac Library, 2005.

**MUSIC**

*Music of Belarus*. Nataliya Romanskaya and Kirmash. Arc Music, 2007.

Music of Belarus (all types of music from modern Belarus). www.belarusguide.com/culture1/music/

# BIBLIOGRAPHY

Ioffe, Grigory. *Understanding Belarus*. Boulder, CO: Rowman & Littlefield Publishers, 2006.

Marples, David R. *Belarus*. Amsterdam: Harwood Academic Publishers, 1999.

Parker, Stewart. *The Last Soviet Republic: Alexander Lukashenko's Belarus*. Victoria, BC: Trafford Publishing, 2007.

Snyder, Timothy. *The Reconstruction of Nations: Poland, Ukraine, Lithuania, Belarus, 1569–1999*. New Haven, CT: Yale University Press, 2004.

White, Stephen, and Elena A. Korosteleva. *Postcommunist Belarus*. Lanham, MD: Rowman & Littlefield Publishers, 2004.

Baltic University Atlas: Belarus. www.balticuniv.uu.se/atlas/belarus/index.htm

BBC History: Joseph Stalin. www.bbc.co.uk/history/historic_figures/stalin_joseph.shtml

BBC News. http://news.bbc.co.uk/1/hi/world/europe/country_profiles/1102180.stm

Belarus—History. www.skiptonps.vic.edu.au/history/belhis.htm

Belarus Miscellany, A: Academics, Essayists, Historians, Novelists, etc. www.belarus-misc.org/writer/bel-writa.htm

Belarus...One More Site About. http://aci.byelarus.com/

Belarus Online: Internet Resources—Business, Media, Photos of Belarus, Belarus People. www.belarus-online.com

Belarusian Telegraph Agency: www.belta.by/en/news/society?id=199032

# BIBLIOGRAPHY

CIA: The World Factbook—Belarus. www.cia.gov/library/publications/the-world-factbook/geos/bo.html#People

Embassy of the Republic of Belarus. www.belarusembassy.org

Encarta: Belarus Facts and Figures. http://encarta.msn.com/fact_631504723/belarus_facts_and_figures.html

Encyclopaedia Britannica: Belavezhskaya Forest. www.britannica.com/eb/topic/60100/Belavezhskaya-Forest

Encyclopaedia Britannica: Dnieper River. www.britannica.com/eb/article-9106069/Dnieper-River#178649.hook

Encyclopaedia Britannica: Dzyarzhynsk Mountain. www.britannica.com/eb/topic-175440/Dzyarzhynsk-Mountain

Encyclopaedia Britannica: Pripet River. www.britannica.com/ebc/article-9375919

Encyclopaedia Britannica: Pripet Marshes. www.concise.britannica.com/ebc/article-9375536/Pripet-Marshes

Encyclopedia of the Nations: Belarus—Education. www.nationsencyclopedia.com/Europe/Belarus-EDUCATION.html

Encyclopedia of the Nations: Belarus—Environment. www.nationsencyclopedia.com/Europe/Belarus-ENVIRONMENT.html

Federation of International Trade Associations: Belarus. www.fita.org/countries/belarus.html

Francis Skaryna. www.belarus-misc.org/writer/skaryna.htm

Francis Skaryna of Polack. www.belarusguide.com/culture1/people/Skaryna.html

History Guide, The: Mikhail Sergeyevich Gorbachev. www.historyguide.org/europe/gorbachev.html

iExplore: Belarus, the Essentials—country and tourist information. www.iexplore.com/dmap/Belarus/The+Essentials

Junior Eurovision Song Contest: 2005. www.youngvoicesstudio.org.uk

Let's Go to...Belarus. www.hotels-europe.com/info-countries/belarus/country.htm

National Parks in Belarus. http://travel.mapsofworld.com/belarus/belarus-tours/national-parks-in-belarus.html

Religion in Belarus. www.belarusguide.com/culture1/religion/Religion.html

Russification. www.historylearningsite.co.uk/russification.htm

Science Daily: Carbon Dioxide Emissions From Power Plants Rated Worldwide. www.sciencedaily.com/releases/2007/11/071114163448.htm

Tiscali.Reference—Belarus. www.tiscali.co.uk/reference/encyclopaedia/countryfacts/belarus.html

United Nations and Chernobyl, The. www.un.org/ha/chernobyl/belarus.html

Virtual Guide to Belarus, The. www.belarusguide.com

# INDEX

airports, 47
architecture, 97, 100, 136
Atlantic Ocean, 8

*babina kasha* (guests), 77
Baltic Sea, 10, 13, 18, 20, 36, 46, 57
Berlin, Irving, 66–67
birthrate, 59
Black Sea, 10, 20, 36, 46, 90
bread, 76, 122, 125–126, 140
    *kalachi*, 126, 140
    rye, 126
Budny, Symon, 66, 90, 104
bus, 47, 69, 71
Byelorussian Soviet Socialist Republic, 24
Bykov, Vasil, 104

Central Berezina Plains, 9, 133
Chagall, Marc, 66, 97–98, 103
children, 52, 74–75, 77, 110
China, 37, 67, 138–139
cities
    Brest, 15
    Gomel, 15
    Grodno, 39, 44, 47, 71, 85, 94, 100, 125, 133, 137
    Minsk, 9, 14, 17–19, 22, 24, 29, 31–32, 37, 40, 44, 47, 51–52, 57, 61–63, 66–67, 70–71, 75, 77–78, 81, 85, 87, 89, 91, 97, 99, 101, 103, 105, 108, 112–113, 123, 133, 136–139
    Navapolatsk, 56
    Pinsk, 18, 67, 93–94, 133, 137
    Polotsk, 9, 18–19, 21–22, 66, 71, 82, 86, 90, 100, 133, 138
    Salihorsk, 56
    Vilnius, 9, 22, 24, 26, 28, 105, 133
    Vitebsk, 17, 19, 22, 47, 62, 67, 71, 83, 98, 133, 137
climate, 5, 8 17, 40, 55
Commonwealth of Independent States (CIS), 14, 37
conservation, 13, 53
crafts, 97, 136
crops
    buckwheat, 42
    flax, 7, 11, 42, 108, 126, 135
    grain, 7
    hemp, 42
    millet, 42, 129
    potatoes, 7, 11, 42, 12–127, 129, 131, 135
    rye, 11, 126
    sugar beets, 42, 135
    tobacco, 42
cultural heritage, 5, 71
Cyrillic alphabet, 90, 92–94

dances, 97
    ballet, 99
    karagods, 118, 140
*dranniki*, 127
drinks
    beer, 112, 129
    *belovezhskaya*, 129, 133
    birch juice, 128
    coffee, 129
    tea, 129

education
    nursery, 70, 75
    primary, 75
    sports, 75
    technical, 61, 75
    universities, 14, 22, 75, 91
        University of Polotsk, 90
    vocational, 75
embroidery, 64–65, 77, 102

factories, 26, 31, 36, 40, 44, 56, 66, 69, 71, 73, 91, 103, 135
families, 40, 61, 73–74, 76, 109, 119
farmland, 7, 49, 51
fertilizers, 15, 40–41, 44, 57
festivals
    Christmas, 67, 83, 118, 120, 121
    Dozinkyoi, 119
    Dzyady, 119
    Easter, 67, 119–121
    Kaliady, 81, 118–121
    Kupalle, 118, 120, 140
    May Day, 122
    Passover, 120, 122
    poetry day, 123
    Radovniza, 119
    Shavuot, 122
    Yom Kippur, 122
fish, 9, 55, 74, 108, 127
flag, 29, 31, 64, 113

forestry, 41
    timber, 10, 15, 44–45
forests, 5, 7, 12–13, 36, 45, 55, 107–109, 118, 125, 136

Germany, 17, 25, 31, 39, 43, 135, 138
glaciers, 7, 9, 140
Gorbachev, Mikhail, 28, 34, 89, 139–140
Great Plain of Eastern Europe, 7, 9
Greenpeace, 53
gross domestic product (GDP), 39

health care, 31, 52, 69, 79
heavy machinery, 44, 50
housing, 31, 70, 78, 100, 108
    dachas, 109
hydroelectric power, 42

ice age, 9, 140
ice cream, 128
iconostasis, 101
independence, 19–20, 24, 28–29, 31–32, 34, 40, 42, 62, 69, 79, 81, 87, 89, 91–92, 95, 110, 117, 122, 135, 139
industrialization, 56, 73
instruments
    accordions, 99
    balalaikas, 99
    cymbals, 99
    lyres, 99
    pipes, 99
IUCN (International Union for the Conservation of Nature), 54

jewelry, 65, 102
judiciary, 34–35, 37

Kazakhstan, 42
Kievan Rus, 18–19, 31, 64, 82
Kolas, Yakub, 104–105
Korbut, Olga, 67, 113
*kotleta pokrestyansky* (pork cutlets), 127
Kupala, Yanka, 104–105, 112, 118

lakes
    Naroch, 10, 133, 137
    Osveyskoye, 10, 133, 137
    Viacha, 7
land reclamation, 11, 56

**143**

language
  Belarusian, 89–95
  English, 115
  Polish, 89–95
  Russian, 89–95
  *Trasyanka*, 94, 140
  Ukrainian, 89–95
  Yiddish, 89–95
Latvia, 7, 43, 133
*ledniks*, 128
life expectancy, 59, 140
literature, 97, 104–105, 123
  *kaski*, 110, 140
Lithuania, 5, 7, 9, 14, 17, 19–22, 24, 26, 28, 31, 37, 42, 47, 71, 82, 84, 90, 115, 133, 138
Lithuanian Statutes of 1557, 21
Lukashenko, Alexander, 5, 29, 32, 39, 113, 139

*machanka*, 127
*magerki* (men's hats), 65
manufacturing, 44, 50, 71
markets, 41, 73, 79, 125, 127
marriages, 74, 76
marshland, 7, 9, 11–12, 45
media, 35, 75, 95, 97, 115
  Internet, 35
  magazines, 35, 61, 115
  newspapers, 35, 62, 115
    *Belaruskaya Delovaya Gazeta*, 115
    *Belorusskaya Niva*, 115
    *Narodnaya Hazeta*, 115
    *Narodnaya Volya*, 115
    *Sovetskaya Belorossiya*, 115
  radio, 35, 75, 99, 115
  television, 35, 44, 67, 71, 107, 110, 114–115, 135
    Belarusian National State Teleradio Company, 114
    NTV, 114
migration, 73
minerals, 44, 135
moraines, 9
mountains
  Dzyarzhynskaya, 9, 137
music, 14, 75, 97, 99, 112, 117, 123, 141
  operas, 99, 115

National Assembly, 32–33
national dress, 64
  *andraki*, 65, 140
national parks, 5, 12, 50, 55
  Belavezhskaya Pushcha, 54–55
  Narochanski, 55
  Pripyatski, 55
  Sosnovy Bor, 53
natural resources, 26, 39, 45, 136
  coal, 10, 42, 45
  dolomite, 45

natural gas, 45, 135
  potash, 45
  oil, 29, 31, 37, 42–43, 45, 82–83, 126, 131, 135, 139
  ore, 10, 45
nature reserves
  Belavezhskaya Forest, 12–13
  Polessky Reserve, 53
  Pripet Nature Reserve, 12, 133
nuclear explosion, 5, 138
  Chernobyl power plant, 5
  radiation, 5, 27, 41, 49–54, 78–79
    leukemia, 51–52

*oblsovet*, 33
Olympics, 67, 113–114

parliament, 31–33
people
  Jews, 21, 59, 62–63, 66, 87, 138
    Poles, 26, 59, 62–63, 71, 84, 139
  Russians, 21, 26, 59–62, 104
  Slavs, 18–19, 92, 138
    Dregovichi, 18, 60
    Drevlyane, 18
    Krivichi, 18, 60, 81, 140
    Radzimichi, 18, 60
  Tatars, 21
  Ukrainians, 21, 59, 63
perestroika, 28, 89, 140
*pirozhki*, 125
Poland, 5, 7, 10, 12, 14–15, 17, 20–22, 24–26, 31, 37, 39, 43, 47, 54, 62, 71, 84–85, 90, 99, 115, 133, 135, 138–139
political parties
  Belarusian Democratic Bloc, 28
  Belarusian Popular Front (BPF), 28
  Green Party, 34
  Liberal Democratic Party, 34
  Nationalist Belarusian Patriotic Party, 34
  Party of Communists of Belarus (PCB), 34
  Social Democratic Gramada, 34
  Socialist Sporting Party, 34
  United Civic Party (UCP), 34
pollution, 49–50, 57
  dichloro-diphenyl-trichloroethane (DDT), 50
  formaldehyde, 50
population, 7, 13–15, 19, 25–26, 39, 59, 62–63, 83–85, 87, 89–90, 94, 103, 127, 137
power stations, 42, 45
Pripet Marshes, 11, 45, 133

railway, 15, 22, 46–47
rainfall, 8
*rayoni*, 33, 140
religion
  Christianity, 18, 61, 81–83, 119

Islam, 87
  Judaism, 87
  Roman Catholicism, 62, 84–85, 87
  Uniate Church, 85
rivers
  Berezina, 9–10, 55, 133, 137
  Bug, 10, 13, 46, 133, 137
  Dnieper, 7, 9–11, 13, 15, 22, 46, 55, 133, 137
  Neman, 9–10, 133, 137
  Oder, 13
  Pripet, 10–12, 45, 108, 133
  Svisloch, 9, 14, 133
  Western Dvina, 10, 133, 137
Russia, 5, 9–10, 17, 21–25, 29, 31, 34, 36–37, 39, 42–43, 47, 53, 60, 64, 67, 69, 71, 92, 95, 98–99, 101, 103, 114, 133, 135–136, 138–139
Russification, 22–23, 59, 61, 90–91, 94, 140

Scherbo, Vitaly, 67, 113
shipping, 10, 46
Shushkevich, Stanislav, 28, 32–33
Skaryna, Francis, 66, 86, 90, 104
socialist realism, 97, 103
soil, 7, 9, 11, 22, 24, 27, 40–41, 50–51, 78–79
soups, 129
sports, 67, 75, 108, 113–114, 129
Stalin, Joseph, 25
Supreme Soviet, 28–29, 32–34
Sweden, 21, 114

theaters, 14, 70, 110, 112
tourism, 39
Treaty of Riga, 24, 138
trees, 8, 12, 45, 55–56

Ukraine, 5, 7, 10–11, 18–19, 21–22, 27, 37, 41, 43, 47, 53, 86, 95, 129, 133, 135, 138
UNESCO (United Nations Educational, Scientific, and Cultural Organization), 13
Union of Lublin, 21–22, 138
United Nations (UN), 49

*voblasti*, 33, 140

water, 7, 50–51, 55–57, 129
wildlife, 5, 7, 11, 13, 53, 55, 107, 109
women, 59, 64–65, 74, 84, 113, 117
woodcarving, 102
World War II, 13–14, 17, 25–26, 40, 44, 56–57, 59, 62, 67, 70–71, 87, 89, 100, 120, 136, 138